iInnovate

iInnovate

A GUIDE FOR ENGAGING IN THE INNOVATION ECONOMY

Randall J. Ottinger

Author of *Beyond Success*

ISBN-13: 9780692735930
ISBN-10: 0692735933

This book is dedicated to my children,
Lauren, Michael, and Ryan,
who inspire me every day,
and bring me joy and optimism for our future.

Table Of Contents

Acknowledgments

There are many people who helped make this book a reality through their research, review, insight, and support. First, I would like to thank my wife, Lea Anne, and daughter, Lauren, for their support. They were my most avid readers, and provided me with many great suggestions. I would also like to thank Vikram Jandhyala and Lara Littlefield from the University of Washington for their support. They have a vast knowledge base into which they allowed me to tap. In addition, I would like to thank Heather Lewis for her support in the research for the book, as well as Joe Kennedy, David Donovick, Lisa Nitze, Peter Nitze, Craig Sherman, Mark Dehmer, Tama Smith, and Lisa Fernow for their review of the manuscript and thoughtful suggestions. Finally, I would like to thank Andrea Kang and Cengiz SARI for their design work.

Introduction

W e are about to embark on a journey of innovation, entre-preneurship, growth, and evolution, but before we do so, some context is important to frame the road ahead. You see, we are truly living in unprecedented times, where there is a convergence of societal needs, technology-enabled solutions, and profitable business approaches. This is creating very large opportunities for companies and communities built on innovation to become powerful forces for positive change.

This convergence did not happen overnight. Quite to the contrary, it has occurred over many decades. Historically, innovation has come in waves as certain breakthroughs have enabled other discoveries to take root. With each technological wave, there have been advances in the way businesses operate and interact with their employees, business partners, and communities.

Today, we are in the midst of a technological wave driven by cheap computer infrastructure accessed through a global network (referred to as cloud computing); nanotechnologies and sensors that allow for monitoring and control of almost everything, including your health, home, security, entertainment, and more (referred to as the Internet of Things); the ability for machines to interact with other machines and learn as they go, which is enabling the feasibility of the driverless car, personalized medicine, and other advances (referred to as machine learning); technology platforms that allow employees, customers, and partners to collaborate and co-create new products and services; and other significant technologies, such as 3-D printing, artificial intelligence, and virtual reality, among others.

As a result of these technological advances, innovation is occurring at an increasingly rapid rate. Global patent filings have grown significantly over the last ten years, and the expansion of Internet access has allowed global collaboration and networks to proliferate. In addition, digital business, which currently accounts for eighteen percent of overall global revenue, is expected to increase to forty-three percent by 2020 according to Gartner Group. The Internet is also enabling many more people to participate in the innovation economy with broad access to ideas, information, money, and other resources.

The organizational changes that will occur as a result of these advances are yet to play out, however, one trend is undeniable, that change is now practically a constant for corporations. In part this is due to the reality that new companies can be created inexpensive by renting computer infrastructure in the cloud, allowing them to quickly build new products and services that leapfrog those offered by established companies. In addition, these smaller competitors are increasingly a threat to incumbents because they can scale globally almost overnight.

To combat these challenges, established companies must become more nimble and innovative. Innovation excellence, which today is already considered one of the most important corporate competencies by leading CEOs, has become even more essential. As technology blurs the boundaries between companies and their customers, business partners, and communities, new innovation related leadership skills are required. Leaders will need to reshape business networks and cultures that engage customers, employees, and other stakeholders in different ways, as partners, which reflects a significant paradigm shift from historic operating models.

Within this global, interconnected reality, companies are seeking top innovation and entrepreneurship talent. They are attempting to shape it from within their companies, as well as to acquire it from the outside. They are also looking to their communities to provide the infrastructure and environment to attract the talent and other resources they will need to grow and succeed.

Urban communities in particular are striving to become innovation and entrepreneurship centers, to attract new talent and companies, and create engines for growth. In addition, they are attempting to build supportive cultures, policies, and even physical spaces that they hope will lead to a virtuous cycle of innovation related benefits for their communities.

Communities that successfully spur the growth of innovation, and build healthy ecosystems that encourage and support start-up companies, are more likely to grow and prosper. As they grow, and employment increases, they receive more tax dollars to invest back into their communities to support education, communications, transportation, healthcare, and other infrastructure. This in turn attracts more people and talent to their communities, leading to even more economic opportunity.

Ultimately, innovation and entrepreneurship communities are becoming "villages of opportunity" as technology related companies create new possibilities for individuals as innovators, entrepreneurs, mentors, lawyers, accountants, educators, consultants, policy makers, intermediaries, nonprofits, and in many other areas.

At the same time, these communities face growing challenges. They need to update their education systems to support the skills required for those desiring to participate in the new job opportunities of the innovation economy; develop new programs to deal with the increased cost of living that is widening the digital divide separating the "haves" and "have-nots" in the innovation economy; address significant employment dislocations due to the displacement of traditional jobs with part-time ones; and improve their start-up ecosystems to enable more entrepreneurs to succeed despite very high failure rates.

In addition, technological advances often lead to unintended consequences and downside scenarios requiring rethinking of policies and regulations. As technology replaces traditional jobs, and we move to a part-time, on-demand, workforce, there are challenges related to the payment of healthcare and other benefits. As more of our private information is made available online, and video surveillance increases, there are questions of how to protect our privacy. As medical advances allow us to live longer, there are also broader ethical and existential issues that surface. These are just a few of the challenges that are surfacing in the innovation economy, and they are growing.

Although these opportunities and challenges frequently appear in the news, many do not understand how the innovation economy works or how best to engage in it. Even those already in the innovation economy frequently touch and understand only a small piece of the total landscape.

iInnovate was written to fill this gap. Through an allegorical tale, it reveals the players and networks that make up the innovation economy, the stages and challenges that exist, and how people can participate in the growing opportunities being created.

So put on your virtual-reality glasses, and let's get started.

Leader To Leader

MILLENNIAL MEETS BABY BOOMER

Liz's heart raced as she scanned the coffee shop. She walked by a couple reading the newspaper and discussing the day's events. Others were holding business conversations in hushed tones. She looked for a man in his mid-fifties by the name of Joe Bloom. She had looked him up on LinkedIn just yesterday. He was somewhat of a legend in the venture capital world, having worked at a number of world-class companies before becoming one of the most well-respected venture capitalists in town. The list of home-run companies he had backed was legendary, and many were now public company powerhouses that had transformed their industries.

Liz was introduced to Joe over e-mail by a mutual friend who indicated that Joe was stepping back from his venture capitalist duties, sitting on boards, increasing his involvement with a number of interesting social enterprises, and occasionally mentoring others looking to connect with the innovation economy.

The innovation economy describes the total economic and social value created by innovation capital investments, including the jobs that are created within companies and communities, and through their networks.

For Liz Li, a twenty-two-year-old student graduating from a state university, college was a blast not only for the friends she made and fun social experiences (which, by the way, were spectacular) but also because she was surrounded by others with a common set of values just like hers. Liz was majoring in earth sciences with a minor in economics. This was considered an interdisciplinary degree, which had become more popular at universities due to the need for solutions that cross fields of study, and work environments requiring collaboration with a wide variety of individuals from different backgrounds and cultures.

As Liz now turned her focus to finding a job in the innovation economy, she longed to work for a company where she could be a catalyst for positive change. It was very important to her, in part because she was bombarded with information all the time about the growing troubles in the world. Information about poverty, climate change, growing health issues, global cultural clashes, security problems, and more were available to her all the time through all kinds of media, including Facebook, Instagram, Twitter, TED Talks, podcasts, and LinkedIn, among other networks and information services. She wanted to help and believed she could in a big way because she was willing to work hard, take risks, and had a voracious curiosity and love of learning.

As Liz's eyes continued to scan the coffee shop, she spotted Joe and recognized him from his profile picture. He was dressed in nice jeans, a button-down shirt, what looked to be expensive shoes, and a sport coat. This is what Liz referred to as "VC chic." It was the look that successful venture capitalists for the most part projected to the outside world to say, "I am still young and hip but also quite financially successful." Or maybe this look had become popular because venture capitalists didn't want to appear conspicuously wealthy and therefore intimidate the very entrepreneurs they most wanted to work with.

Joe was sitting with someone she did not recognize, also in his fifties, however, this other person was dressed more formally in a suit and tie. When she approached the table, Joe put out his hand to greet her, saying, "Hi, you must be Liz. Bill told me many good things about you. I understand you are just graduating from college and are exploring career opportunities. I would like to introduce you to Rick Valdez. Rick has been an executive at an energy company and is also looking at his next career opportunity. Rick has vast experience in the environment, energy, and sharing economy, and I thought it would be useful for you to meet Rick, given my understanding of your interests in these areas."

"Thank you, Joe," said Liz, "and nice to meet you, Rick. I am very appreciative that you would take the time to sit down with me given your busy schedules. The truth is, I am graduating soon and need some advice on my first real career move. I could use your counsel,

Joe, as someone who has walked down the innovation and entrepreneurship path many times before."

"Liz," replied Joe, "it is my pleasure to help. So much has been given to me during my life, and I very much want to give back by helping entrepreneurs like you and executives in transition, like Rick, who want to be part of the innovation economy."

"It is a pleasure for me to meet you as well," said Rick. "I have children around your age and am finding I am learning a lot from them these days. It is going to be fun for me to hear more about you, and I am happy to share my experience as well. I have had a more traditional business background. After business school, I joined a large energy company. My background is in engineering, and I started working in their manufacturing plants. There I learned about supply chains, management practices, and manufacturing automation. Then I worked in their labs evaluating new technologies for manufacturing and for low-cost energy solutions.

"I am now interested in identifying ways I can be involved in endeavors that improve the environment and communities. I have just started to investigate ways to work with our community planners, university researchers, and even some nonprofits that support this area of focus. At this stage of my career, I care more about improving our community and environment than making tons of money, though I still do need to work."

Jumping in with a probing question that took the conversation quickly from 0 to 60 miles per hour, Joe asked, "Liz, what motivates you at this point in your life?"

"I want to make a difference in the world and for my work to matter. I believe in myself and my abilities to help a company be successful, and I know in the end that it will lead to financial benefits for me. Although making a lot of money is not my first priority, I do want to make a good living and have the flexibility to enjoy my life, travel, and share fun experiences with friends. No offense, but I have seen how older generations have slaved away and in some ways forgotten to live their lives. I don't want this to happen to me. I am willing to work hard, but I don't want to spend too long toiling in the bowels of a large company on things that aren't considered important.

"Ultimately, I believe that I can run my own company, and truthfully that is my dream. Similar to Rick, I would be very excited to work on solutions in the sharing economy and that improve the environment. I believe my skills and interests would be best suited for these opportunities, and a number of my classes have provided me with background in these areas, which I found fascinating."

"Liz, have you considered opportunities in the government or nonprofit sectors?" asked Joe.

Liz mused, "I have thought about this, but to be honest, I do not know enough about government opportunities to give you an informed answer. For the most part, I have not seen a well-functioning government during my lifetime. Also, I am not sure I have the stomach to work through the bureaucracy required to achieve meaningful impact in the government.

"Separately, although I have friends who have graduated and gone down the nonprofit road and seem very fulfilled, I find the business world more exciting. It seems most nonprofits have difficulty scaling and sustaining themselves in the same way as for-profit companies. My ideal career opportunity would allow me to help build a company that improves lives. I am just not sure of the best way to go about it."

The conversation continued on in this manner for most of the hour, with Joe asking probing questions and Liz and Rick answering from their unique perspectives. The more they spoke, the more Rick and Liz determined they had a lot of complementary skills. Rick had valuable business experience in areas in which Liz was interested. Liz, on the other hand, had a great deal of current knowledge, enthusiasm, and determination to build a company.

"As I listen to you both," said Joe, "it appears to me you have similar motivations to improve lives, and there is some overlap in terms of your areas of interest in the environment and sharing economy.

On the other hand, Liz, you want to pursue entrepreneurial business opportunities in this area, and Rick, you have a broader community interest. Do I have that right?"

Liz and Rick both nodded.

"Well, that is good background information and will allow me to introduce you to people who can inform you about the roles, challenges, and opportunities in these areas."

Looking at his watch, Joe realized the hour had quickly passed. He suggested that they meet again the following week. "At that time, I will lay out the innovation journey for you."

Insights about Millennials and Baby Boomers

- There are sixty million millennials (born between 1980 and 1995). They now make up the largest share of the labor market.[1]
- Sixty-six percent of millennials expect to leave their current employer within the next five years, and work-life balance takes precedence over career progression.[2]
- Sixty-two percent of millennials want to work for a company that makes a positive impact. Fifty percent of millennials prefer purposeful work to a high salary, and 53 percent would work harder if they were making a difference to others.[3]
- There are seventy-six million baby boomers (born between 1946 and 1964). According to demographic data, by 2029 all the baby boomers will be sixty-five years or older, which will cause one of the largest brain drains that the US workforce has ever seen.[4]
- Millennials are turning increasingly to baby boomers for advice and mentorship. Sixty-five percent of baby boomers indicate that millennials have sought them out for guidance.[5]

The Innovation Journey

THE STAGES AND CHALLENGES OF INNOVATION, ENTREPRENEURSHIP, GROWTH, AND EVOLUTION

A week later, Liz arrived at the coffee house early and sat down at the table where Joe, Rick, and she last met. She had a cup of piping-hot black coffee for Rick and a macchiato for Joe. Buying coffee was a small gesture of thanks from Liz.

A coffee house was like Liz's office away from school, where she could get her work done without feeling like she was at a library. There was a bit of socializing and a buzz of energy, probably enhanced by the coffee!

Rick arrived first, followed by Joe five minutes later. Joe seemed quite energized and approached the table with swift steps. He grabbed the coffee from Liz, said a quick 'thank you', and without skipping a beat started in.

"Liz and Rick," he said, "since we last met, I decided to bring a map I put together awhile ago that is an overview of the innovation journey. As I mentioned last time, it outlines the challenges that business and community leaders face at different stages in their life-cycle, the interactions that occur between companies and their communities along the way, and the networks that support their success.

"As we travel on this journey together, I will introduce you to Jean Patel, the founder of VT Corp., one of the portfolio companies I invested in that has now become a global leader in transportation safety products and services for the driverless car. She can describe to you her career and the road that led to creating one of the most admired public companies in this area.

"I will also introduce you to Tom Sorenson, a former business executive and community leader, who has been involved in building our innovation economy for as long as I can remember. Tom and Jean have seen their community and company grow up together and can provide perspectives on each stage of the journey."

Liz couldn't stop looking at the paper rolled up in Joe's hand, and wondering what was written on it. Joe held it like it was the map to some great treasure. Maybe it was, but Joe was not going to show it to Liz or Rick before he shared some background knowledge first.

"Before we start the journey," said Joe, "I would like to highlight an important distinction between an innovation company and a technology company. In some ways, all companies are a hybrid of technology and business practices. Some companies use technologies to enhance their businesses, while others sell technologies but face the same business challenges as their nontechnology peers. All companies, however, go through the same business stages, beginning with an entrepreneur taking a risk to start a business, then growing it, and ultimately passing it along to his or her family members, management team, employees, or selling it.

"The real difference between technology companies and non-technology companies is that true technology companies face constant change from the day they start, while many companies in more mature industries have been insulated from such rapid change. This, however, is quickly morphing as even companies in the most insulated of industries are facing accelerated changes due to technological advances and globalization.

"In my opinion, innovation companies that are able to swiftly harness and implement new ideas, effectively use technologies in the pursuit of their business objectives, and build cultures that empower their employees to be leaders at all levels, will adapt and thrive. The same is true of innovation communities. Those that build the infrastructure and culture for innovation and entrepreneurship to thrive will flourish, and other communities will die away."

At this point, Joe started to unroll the scroll while Liz and Rick looked on with anticipation. Joe put salt and pepper shakers on one end of the scroll and searched for a sugar container to place on the other end. With the scroll displayed flat on the table, Joe began...

"This map provides a bird's-eye view of the innovation journey. It outlines the business leaders and key challenges they face at different points in the journey, as well as the internal and external business and community networks that form over time."

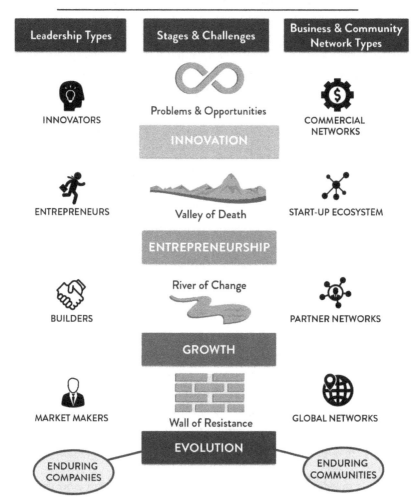

"What stands out to you as you look at this map?" asked Joe.

"Well, there appear to be four stages of the journey, including innovation, entrepreneurship, growth, and evolution. As you move through these stages it appears that the leadership types, key challenges at each stage, and networks supporting companies seem to change," said Liz.

"Good observations," confirmed Joe. "Business leaders face different challenges, attempt to accomplish distinct milestones, and need unique kinds of support at each stage of the journey. This presents significant difficulties for company leaders as they grow.

"During the innovation stage, innovators seek to overcome specific problems they see in the world or opportunities they can exploit in the market. They hope to identify new technologies that will allow for great leaps forward in our knowledge and capabilities. Their success is measured by the intellectual property they create, which in many cases can be commercialized, however, in other cases lead to advances in our knowledge and understanding in a wide variety of areas.

"During the entrepreneurial or start-up stage, founders of companies strive to create financial value from new and innovative solutions. Entrepreneurs can be the founders of technology or more traditional companies. Their most significant challenge is to raise enough funding to build the foundation of a company that fills a real market need so they don't end up in the Valley of Death. This is a common term describing the high mortality rate of start-ups that are undercapitalized and run out of funding. Entrepreneurs often look to a start-up ecosystem of advisors, mentors, and seed funders, to help them successfully navigate this stage.

"The growth stage of companies is led by business builders, and this stage is marked by the need to scale quickly. Growth companies face a river of almost constant change as they scale, hire new employees, and expand into new geographies, products, and services. In order to grow quickly they develop a network of partners that help them scale in many areas. These partners become a strategic advantage for these companies, and barriers against competition.

"Finally, the evolution stage is marked by successful companies that are able to overcome a wall of resistance from established players and their partners. These market makers break through the wall of resistance, and are able to continuously innovate and evolve to build enduring companies. This is no easy task for a large and oftentimes global company, and many fail as they expand into new geographies. Their success again relies on a global network of partners with localized knowledge and expertise."

Rick broke in saying, "One other thing that stands out to me on this map is your emphasis on business and community networks. Given that there are so many other factors that make for a successful company, why is this such a focus of yours?"

"You are correct, there are many factors that lead to successful companies, but networks are increasingly one of the most critical for long-term success. While certain other barriers against competition, such as intellectual property and patents, are becoming harder to create and defend in many areas, networks and relationships, enabled by technology, are increasingly important for sustained company and community success. They allow for better communications, collaboration, co-creation of solutions with stakeholders, and sustained innovation.

"A second reason for focusing on networks is that many jobs that exist in the innovation economy are contained in these networks. In other words, jobs are not only created in start-up companies but also in the business and community networks that support them. We will explore these connections and networks in more detail at each stage of the journey."

Rick followed up with another observation, "In my experience, companies and communities don't step back to view the entire journey but rather focus on the stage they are in. Why is this?"

"That is a good insight, and I believe there are a number of reasons this is so. First, the challenges at each stage are so acute that it is difficult for companies to look too far ahead. When you consider the high rate of failure at each stage of the journey, it is no surprise why there is a need to focus on the stage one is in. Studies show, for instance, that a high majority of start-ups fail within the first few years, and very few grow to have greater than five hundred employees. Even the most successful companies on the Fortune 500 list are falling out quicker than ever before.

"In addition, investors in particular reinforce the focus on the stage in which they have invested because they are measured by the increase in value they are able to create within that stage. Their hope is to sell to others who focus on a later stage so they can monetize the value created by their portfolio of companies."

"You mentioned the high failure rate of start-ups. What are the key drivers of the high failure rate, and how do companies overcome them?" asked Liz.

"As we go on the innovation journey we will answer this question for each specific stage, however, in brief, a major driver of the high failure rate relates to leadership and the need for new leadership practices. If you consider that technology will create many jobs in the future that don't yet exist today, that new companies can scale globally almost overnight, and that talent is available to companies anywhere in the world from the moment they start, you can imagine that new leadership practices will be required at all stages.

"In terms of leadership," continued Joe, "accompanying us on the innovation journey will be two leaders who were involved from the very start in building a great company and community that grew up together. We will meet them the next time we get together."

Joe suggested they meet at his office the next week to start on what he termed their "virtual journey," which intrigued both Liz and Rick a great deal.

Insights about the Challenges of the Innovation Journey

- Most companies fail within the first three years.[6]
- Less than 2 percent of all companies grow to have more than five hundred employees.[7]
- The average life span of a company on the S&P 500 has decreased from ninety years in 1935 to eighteen years today. At the current churn rate, 75 percent of S&P 500 companies will be removed from the index by 2027.[8]
- To reach an audience of fifty million people, it took radio thirty-eight years, the Internet four years, and Angry Birds thirty-five days.[9]
- Sixty-five percent of grade-school children will go into jobs that don't exist today and for which they cannot be trained.[10]
- Success in the digital future will depend on a company's ability to implement digital technologies that support innovation.[11]

Sparking The Innovation Engine

ENABLING RESEARCH, INVENTION, AND COMMERCIALIZATION

L iz and Rick were ushered into a conference room at Joe's offices, where Joe was fiddling around with virtual-reality glasses. He looked up to greet them when they entered the room.

"Welcome to my offices. I am just trying out these virtual-reality glasses. If you put them on, I will introduce you to Jean, who is waiting for us in the place where she developed the initial prototypes for VT Corp."

Rick and Liz had both heard of Jean and VT Corp. The company was one of the first to develop sensors and other components for self-driving cars. As the company grew, it became the leader in this area, and it was now the largest employer in the community.

When Rick and Liz put on their glasses, they were virtually transported to what appeared to be a machine shop, or what is termed today a "maker space." Within a very large room, there were all kinds of equipment, including 3-D printers, digital-design workstations, and much more. In the midst of a lot of activity, there stood Jean, going from person to person to find out what everyone was working on. When Liz, Rick, and Joe entered the room, Jean was notified to put on her own virtual-reality glasses.

Jean greeted Liz and Rick and let them know how supportive Joe had been as an investor in VT Corp. and as an adviser to Jean. She said how happy she was to tell them her story about VT Corp., how it was founded, quickly grew, and ultimately went public.

"To go back to the beginning," started Jean, "I conceived of the idea for our company when I was a student at our state research university. You see, I was an engineering major and had taken a number of classes on the future of transportation. There I learned about the driverless car, and we had a class about the challenges facing its adoption. One of those challenges was how to ensure passenger safety in a driverless environment.

"One of my professors was fond of saying that good solutions come from clearly identifying problems to overcome. The driverless car offered the hope of a more efficient way of commuting with fewer accidents, better use of our roads, and potentially less pollution. The problem I was interested in addressing was how to ensure passenger safety in self-driving cars under an almost unlimited number of scenarios.

"It seemed to me addressing this enormous problem had great commercial potential, but I was not able to predict the timing of demand, which is so essential for any new company. Some say that the timing of the introduction of a new innovation is a very large predictor of success, and many ideas are introduced before the market is ready. In addition, at that time there were many different approaches for tackling driverless car safety, and I was not sure which solution would be the one that car companies would adopt. My greatest lesson at this stage was how critical it is to clearly define problems, which leads to better solutions for addressing customer needs."

"So did you start the company at school?" asked Rick.

"Well, the initial concepts were developed at school. The university had investment dollars they provided to a group of us that allowed us to hack together some preliminary concepts that we were interested in developing. With that money, we were also able to buy some first-generation sensors and begin developing the software that was to become the automobile safety nerve center for the driverless car.

"In addition, we learned a lot by trying to develop our initial solution, but clearly it was a bigger deal than we first thought. Also, I did not feel I had the skills to start a company at that time, and instead I joined one of the major car companies in town. The car company had an R&D lab, and one of the areas they were funding was initial research in the area of self-driving cars. After working in the car company's manufacturing plants awhile, I joined this R&D lab. In fact, this is the lab where a team of us put together the initial prototypes for the self-driving car, though there was a lot less equipment to play with back then."

"So why didn't the car company want to own this technology and build a division to develop these safety components and the software for the driverless car nerve center?" asked Rick.

"The truth is that I pitched this to the car company execs, but they had other investments they wanted to make in solutions with a shorter term payback," answered Jean. "As you know, all companies face the reality that they need to prioritize their development efforts because they have limited funds to invest. We would have had to license anything we had developed at the car company, but when we left we decided on a different design than the one we developed there. Still, we had to get their written permission to start the company before I left so they would not be able to claim any rights to the intellectual property we were soon to create."

"So is this when you started your company?" asked Liz.

"Yes. A number of us actually left the car company to start VT Corp., but in reality, we were totally focused on developing the initial products and not building our company. We were pre–start-up, if you will. I was more or less what you would call the product manager, and there were two brilliant engineers who came with me. We felt we could build the initial components and software, and had enough knowledge about the industry to believe the timing was right. Executives from our former employer, the car company, even suggested they would be our first customer if we could raise the money to build a working prototype. That is when I met Joe."

Joe chimed in, "Jean and her team were innovators and had great technical expertise, however, they had not yet developed enough of a founding team with the entrepreneurial talent we typically look for in a start-up. Like many venture capital firms, we typically wait to invest until there is a product to sell and proof of the market need from paying customers. In addition, although VT Corp.'s leadership team had the technical expertise to develop their solution, nobody in the company at that time had any start-up business experience. As a result, instead of investing, we connected Jean to a local incubator and some wealthy angel investors who ultimately invested enough money so Jean could continue working on the product."

"Is Jean's scenario typical of the way start-ups are founded?" asked Liz.

"There are a number of start-up scenarios I have seen over the years," answered Joe. "Jean's scenario is fairly typical for a company founded by an innovator. Many innovators have an inventor's mentality. They develop a focused expertise around a science or technology that allow them to have the insights required to develop new inventions. They are good at innovating, but they frequently must partner with entrepreneurs with business experience to help them build companies based on their inventions.

"Unlike most innovators, entrepreneurs are business risk takers with the ability to build leadership teams, attract capital, and win initial customers. Some are technical as well, with the skills to develop solutions themselves, although many look to partner with or contract out technical talent. We will address these scenarios further when we talk about entrepreneurship."

At that moment, another person appeared in the lab. He was tall and in his sixties. It was Tom, the community leader whom Joe had spoken about. Tom Lincoln had been a leader in the community for decades and was involved in many of the decisions that led the community to become an innovation center.

Tom started by saying, "Let me apologize for being late, but my meeting ran over and I could not find my virtual-reality glasses. I know a great deal about Jean's story and the founding of VT Corp. Joe asked me to describe what we were working on with the mayor at the time VT Corp. was founded. Is now a good time for me to talk about this?"

Joe and Jean indicated this was a good time.

"As background, I am part of a community leadership council that has worked collaboratively to develop policies and priorities to attract researchers, inventors, and start-up companies to our city. The council includes the mayor and his heads of innovation and economic development; leaders of major companies, including the car company Jean worked for; the vice provost for innovation and tech transfer at our state university; and a number of community and nonprofit leaders.

"Our initial discussions and focus were on the values, principles, and goals we all could rally around to build the community we wanted. Just like companies have cultures, communities have cultures as well. For communities to achieve robust innovation and start-up success requires a culture of risk taking and tolerance of failure. Communities must also decide that they want to grow, and many communities determine they like things the way they have always been. Our community, however, wanted to grow, so we looked at how to leverage the institutions that were pillars of the community at that time. What may not be obvious to you is that Jean used many resources from institutions that were funded by the government and community to build her know-how and initial solutions."

Jean nodded in agreement.

"At that time," continued Tom, "our priority was to help build one of the most highly respected state research universities. Every community we studied that became an innovation center had a strong research university as one of its pillars. We pushed for as much federal funding as we could to hire top professors, develop curricula, and build maker spaces at the university. In particular, we focused on hiring top professors in science, technology, engineering, and math, as well as researchers in areas that were strategic to the community. Jean took advantage of these resources while at the university, as I am sure she mentioned.

"The state university also hired a head of innovation and tech transfer to partner with major companies and investment firms in the community. The charter of that group, along with the deans of the individual departments, was to help students and faculty develop, patent, and license technology, as well as create strong partnerships with companies, investment firms, government agencies, and nonprofits in the community to fund research and company spinouts. The tech transfer office also had access to a pool of money to fund new ideas that were developed by faculty and students, which Jean also used while at school."

"You mentioned you focused on funding in areas that were strategic to the community," commented Rick. "How did you determine what was strategic?"

"The city conducted a study of the strategic advantages of our community and determined that, given our location in the middle of the country and the fact that we had a number of highly successful automobile and logistics companies, one strategic area of opportunity was in the transportation area. Our community had a cluster of successful transportation companies and a network of related suppliers and distributors that had grown organically to support them. As a result, the established transportation companies in our community became a second pillar we could leverage.

"Also, although automobile and logistics companies are in established industries, the companies in our community were actively looking for ways to reinvent themselves. They were hiring engineers and technology talent at a rapid rate and were also funding research, which created quite a bit of synergy with our state university research. In fact, the R&D lab at the car company where Jean worked conducted a lot of collaborative research with the university.

"In addition, another influential innovation pillar at that time was our supportive government, led by the mayor, who actively brought together leaders from the university, city planning, real estate, and private sector to help frame the policies, develop the planning for infrastructure and physical spaces, and attract the funding to leverage our geographic advantages. As a result of their collaborative efforts, we not only attracted government and other funding for innovation, we also attracted core innovation talent to our city, including researchers, technologists, professors, and inventors. They have been directly involved in patenting transportation and other related technologies."

"Where did the investment come from to fund innovation in the community, and how did you measure whether you were being successful in building a strong innovation community?" asked Rick.

"Most of the R&D dollars for innovation in our community, as is true in the rest of the United States, came from corporations through their R&D initiatives, followed by the federal government, which funded researchers and innovators at our university. In addition, it turns out the transportation sector is one of the most R&D-intensive industries, and we found that the transportation companies in our community were investing heavily in R&D. Also, some of our wealthier individuals in the private sector funded innovation through their family offices.

"In terms of measurement, a great deal of focus has been on R&D spending and the number of patents created, which is not a perfect proxy for innovation but is frequently used. Many jobs have been created as a result of R&D spending, and they are leveraged when inventions are then commercialized. This initial cycle of innovation and start-up activity is important for an enduring community, and without it we would not be in the position we are today."

Joe indicated that, as the discussion was moving from innovation to commercialization, this seemed like a good time to talk about the second stage of the journey: entrepreneurship, with a focus on start-ups. And with a wave of his hand, the current scene faded away and was gradually replaced by a new one.

Insights about Innovation

- The United States remained the world's top "inventive country" in 2014, accounting for 28.6 percent of all international patent applications, followed by Japan, China, Germany, and South Korea.[12]
- In 2015, the United States led the world in R&D expenditures as well, followed by China, Japan, Germany, and South Korea.[13]
- The rate of US R&D expenditures as a percentage of gross domestic product, however, ranks the United States eighth in the world.[14]
- Innovation capital amounts to $14 trillion across sixteen countries. This is equivalent to 42 percent of their gross domestic product.[15] Analysis of the relationship between innovation capital and economic development indicates that innovation directly contributed to 53 percent of labor productivity growth.[16]
- In 2015, total US R&D expenditures were expected to be $496 billion, with the majority coming from corporations, followed by federal government spending.[17]
- In 2015, the federal government was estimated to have invested $136 billion in research, with over half going to the Department of Defense.[18]
- The global industries that spend the most on R&D are the computing and electronics, health care, and auto sectors. They account for 62 percent of total global innovation spending. The health-care sector is expected to be the largest spender by 2019. [19]
- American universities occupy nine of the top ten and twenty-eight out of the top fifty rankings in international patent filings by educational institutions.[20]

Guiding Entrepreneurs Through The Valley Of Death

CREATING START-UP COMPANIES AND COMMUNITIES

Jean, Joe, Liz, and Rick found themselves in a convention center watching eight entrepreneurs preparing to give a presentation to a group of angel investors. Jean's partner, Dave Shapiro, was one of the entrepreneurs who had made the presentation for Jean's company many years ago. In fact, they met at this same accelerator that had prepared the eight presenters for this day.

Accelerators are organizations that help entrepreneurs develop their business plans and pitches to investors over a three- to four-month time frame working with cohort groups of ten to twelve people. They offer mentorship and educational elements, and culminate in a public pitch event for investors.

When Dave met Jean, he had already been a serial entrepreneur, having started a number of successful companies. He now hung around the accelerator to be a resource and mentor to others and to look at ideas for his next entrepreneurial venture. Jean and Dave hit it off immediately, and Jean brought Dave in as a cofounder of VT Corp.

"When I met Dave," said Jean, "I had hit the wall. The initial innovation stage of our company was quite intense. I was developing our initial driverless car software platform and components, trying to raise money to complete the products, and hiring to enhance our development team, all at the same time. I was also very well aware that most start-up companies fail within their first three years, and I did not want to be one of those statistics. I knew I needed help, and I wanted to set the company up for success from the outset. Dave had complementary skills that I did not have, and we felt that together we could raise enough money to cross the Valley of Death."

"So why do they call it the Valley of Death?" asked Rick, not familiar with this term from his corporate background.

"'Valley of Death' is a term that is used by the start-up community to describe the early stages of a company when it runs out of money as it moves from innovation to commercialization," said Jean. "That is where I was heading before I met Dave. I had done the research on the driverless car, developed the technical specifications for the initial products, and raised a little money from friends and family to build the initial prototype. After a while, however, I found I was running out of money and had way too much on my plate.

Crossing the Valley of Death (Accomplishing the 4Cs)

"Dave was an absolute godsend," continued Jean, "and together we set out to accomplish four key milestones. I call them the "4Cs", because they relate to capital, customers, culture and talent, and connections."

Liz raised her eyebrows and looked over toward Dave as if to say, "You take it from here."

"Jean had a big vision for the products she wanted to offer," said Dave, "but it would have taken way too long and cost too much money to develop. As a result, we agreed on what is termed a 'minimal viable product' that we could develop and customers could purchase.

"A minimal viable product or service has basic functionality that allows a new company to pursue initial customers and prove there is a market need for what they have developed. In the past, there was a long research phase before developing and bringing a product to market. Today, it is often cheaper and quicker to build a basic product, try to sell it, and then iterate with customer feedback, depending of course on the industry.

"With our minimal viable product we were able to accomplish our first milestone," continued Dave, "which was to identify early customers that would be willing to try the product with the intent to purchase. A product manager at the car company where Jean formerly worked raised his hand to be one of our initial customers. As Jean said, the car company was not able to invest enough to develop products in this area itself, and in many ways, it was easier for them to work with a young company that could build a solution that met its needs.

Early customers are critical for start-up companies to prove their business thesis, including validating that there is actually demand and a willingness to pay for their solutions.

"The second milestone we focused on was to build a top founding team with technical and business skills, which we did in part by creating an engaging culture. Not all business leaders are meant to be entrepreneurs. It is highly stressful, and entrepreneurs have to be comfortable with quickly changing direction based on customer feedback, without being reactionary of course.

"They are also constantly raising money while at the same time operating the business. As Joe may have mentioned, between Jean and I, we checked most of the boxes our initial outside investors were looking for in a leadership team, but we needed to supplement the team with some seasoned sales and marketing talent. The culture we created allowed us to attract the talent we needed."

Dave continued, "One of the biggest problems many entrepreneurs face, which we were able to avoid, is that they run out of money before they can complete these milestones. This can happen for a number of reasons, including the initial idea was not exactly right or the company had to go through too many iterations before hitting on the right set of features and business approach.

"The iterations and changes of direction companies go through are commonly referred to in the industry as 'pivoting'. The dilemma is that while entrepreneurs are iterating on the product and business model, many run out of cash. Unfortunately, it is futile to look for growth investors, such as venture capitalists, until these milestones are accomplished, and companies can just run out of options, becoming a statistic in the 'Valley of Death'.

"What a shame and waste of time, money, and talent to see so many start-ups fail," said Rick.

"Yes and no," said Joe. "This is the way innovation works, and the United States is one of the best countries at it, enabling the free flow of talent and money to ideas. In fact, in communities like Silicon

Valley there is a culture where failure is tolerated, and sometimes even a badge of experience that investors seek, though most would say it is better to learn from success rather than failure whenever possible."

"So how were you able to cross the Valley of Death? What actions did you take? And who finally invested in you?" asked Liz.

Jean took the question by saying, "In short, with a minimal viable product, customers willing to purchase it, and a strong leadership team, we determined that we had the elements needed to attract willing investors. In order to identify investors and approach them with credibility, however, we knew we needed to leverage our connections. We did this by thoughtfully building a strong founding group that included board members, mentors, professional advisers, and others who we identified as key advocates for the company."

"So how did you put your founding group together, and where did they come from?" asked Liz.

"First, our main objective was to identify the players who would be most strategic and active in helping us," said Dave. "We wrote down the key roles we wanted to fill, including our initial investors, board members, and professional legal and financial advisers. We knew we wanted supporters who were well connected to investors and prospective customers, and had special insights and relationships in the transportation industry where we were going to compete. We also wanted supporters who would be active in helping us achieve our key milestones. We learned that this was more important than identifying famous or successful people with big titles.

"In terms of where we found these supporters, some came from our personal connections, but many came through the contacts we made through our accelerator. We found that incubators and accelerators, such as this one, already have assembled a large entrepreneurial support network to choose from. Dave came to know the incubators, accelerators, angel investors, and other start-up support organizations in town as a result of the companies he had started, and he valued their advice and networks.

"As background, incubators and accelerators provide start-ups with shared space, services, and a network of investors, mentors, and professionals. Their objective is to help entrepreneurs prepare their companies to raise seed capital, and some even provide a little funding themselves. One significant area of value they provide is to allow entrepreneurs with similar challenges to network with and learn from one another as well as from seasoned mentors.

"Most entrepreneurs spend between four and twelve months at an accelerator or incubator. The pitches to a broad network of advisers and angel investors, like the ones you see behind us, are from entrepreneurs who are graduating from the accelerator's program. This accelerator is not only where Dave and I met each other, but is also where we were introduced to our first investors and board members.

"In healthy innovation communities, you see many incubators, accelerators, angel networks, and other types of organizations like these that support start-up companies. In addition, these organizations are often linked as part of a broader start-up ecosystem, and you frequently run into the same people at meet-ups and conferences."

"I have a clarifying question," interjected Rick, "which is, how are angel investors and networks different from incubators and accelerators?"

"Angels are wealthy individuals who like investing in start-ups or early stage companies," said Dave. "Many enjoy being mentors, advisers, or board members, and also like the stimulation of evaluating deals together with other wealthy investors. This is one reason why angel-investor networks have formed. In fact, angel networks have become quite sophisticated in their investment approach. Similar to venture capitalists, many conduct deep due diligence on companies to make sure they meet key criteria prior to bringing them in front of their angel-investor networks.

"In addition, angel-investor networks, like incubators and advisers, can also help their companies with investor pitches. The pitches to angel investors are typically very short, often ten to fifteen minutes including questions. Interested investors are then provided with a detailed package and business plan about the company, market, competition, product or service, customer pipeline, business model, and valuation, among other information."

"So did you find it to be an advantage starting VT Corp. in this community with a strong start-up ecosystem?" asked Liz. "Also, what if you don't live in a community with a robust start-up ecosystem?"

"Well, great entrepreneurs can start companies anywhere, but it is just much easier to do so in healthy start-up communities," commented Joe. "Start-up communities, networks, and ecosystems are receiving increased attention because they are engines for economic development and can create a competitive advantage for local communities. It doesn't mean you can't start a successful company in another community, but it is just much harder to do."

At this point, Tom, who had been listening to the conversation until now, spoke up.

Building a Strong Start-Up Ecosystem

"As Jean and Dave indicated, creating a strong start-up ecosystem can lead to more new companies, greater employment, and strong economic development. Let me tell you how we went about creating the start-up ecosystem in our community, and why this is now a great place to start a company.

"As we discussed, our community spent time in the past building strong innovation pillars, including our state university, supportive government, and major corporations, and we turned to them again to collaborate around the need and opportunity to help new companies get started. Each of these pillars could see the benefits of more start-ups from their own perspective and were willing to be supportive.

"Our state university saw that it could benefit from helping faculty and students start companies on campus with university resources. It decided to create its own incubator and allocate shared start-up space for students, professors, and alumni. The university received investment capital from alumni to not only build and maintain the space but also fund a certain number of start-ups from the university incubator each year.

"In addition, the university added professors and curricula to their entrepreneurship programs for students and executives. They collaborated wherever they could with community institutions promoting entrepreneurship. For instance, they invited investment firms in to mentor students and judge new business contests. Students were also provided opportunities to work with venture capitalists and local companies as interns to learn about starting and growing companies.

"In a mature start-up ecosystem, there is significant collaboration between start-up investors, academics, entrepreneurs, professional advisers, government agencies, and even nonprofits. They all know one another, attend start-up events together, and share opportunities and lessons learned with one another. Some would call great start-up communities boundariless because they operate across silos that exist in this environment. Most participants in a start-up ecosystem care about improving the start-up community in addition to their own personal interests."

"What role did corporations and the government play in building a successful start-up ecosystem?" asked Rick.

"The major corporations in our community were interested in mentoring students and providing internships as a way to identify employee talent early. One company even funded a start-up contest to identify and fund projects in areas where they had a strategic interest.

"As for the government, it created incentives for wealthy individuals to invest in early-stage companies and in return receive some tax breaks. It also encouraged real-estate developers to create shared incubation space and in return receive zoning concessions from the government. Finally, our community has a very favorable tax structure for small, early-stage companies that not only helped to lower barriers for starting companies but also attracted early-stage companies from other regions."

"How did you measure the success of your start-up efforts?" asked Rick.

"During this stage of our community's lifecycle we were focused on increasing the number of start-up companies in our area, and creating new employment opportunities at start-ups. We successfully accomplished these objectives, and, in addition, grew the number of institutions supporting start-ups, such as incubators, accelerators, and organized seed-capital firms. A number of angel networks and a seed fund were also formed at this time, which was critically important. Organized capital for funding start-ups is another pillar you will find in a healthy start-up ecosystem."

"As a number of these start-ups succeeded and began to quickly grow, what challenges did they face?" asked Liz.

"That is a great question and brings us to the next stage of the journey: the growth stage. Let me suggest that we take a break and then reconvene to talk about how the needs of companies and communities morph as they grow and face a 'river of change.'"

Insights about Entrepreneurship

- There were over 530,000 new business owners every month during 2015.[21]
- Thirty-three percent of new entrepreneurs are college graduates. The top five universities graduating successful entrepreneurs are Stanford, UC Berkley, University of Pennsylvania, Harvard, and MIT.[22]
- New entrepreneurs in the United States are becoming increasingly diverse, with more than 40 percent of new entrepreneurs being composed of African American, Latino, Asian, or other nonwhite entrepreneurs. Immigrant entrepreneurs now account for 28.5 percent of all new entrepreneurs in the United States.[23]
- Most new entrepreneurs in 2015 were male, making up 63.2 percent of all new entrepreneurs. Since 1997, the percentage of new female entrepreneurs has fallen from 43.7 percent to 36.8 percent.[24]
- The amount of young entrepreneurs (ages twenty to thirty-four) is on the decline. Entrepreneurs backed by venture capitalists are older (48 percent are between thirty-five and forty-four), more experienced (on average, they have worked for a company eight years before starting a venture), and have been entrepreneurs before (39 percent were former founders or CEOs).[25]
- The ten highest valued start-ups in April 2016 as determined by venture capitalists are Uber, Xiaomi, Airbnb, Palantir, Meituan-Dianping, Snapchat, WeWork, Didi Kuaidi, Flipkart, and SpaceX.[26]
- The number of US-based accelerators grew from sixteen programs in 2008 to twenty-seven in 2009 and forty-nine in 2010, before eventually reaching 170 programs in 2014, an

annual average growth of 50 percent per year between 2008 and 2014.[27]

- The top start-up accelerators as ranked by Rice University, MIT, and the University of Richmond in 2016 are 500 Startups, Alchemist, Amplify LA, AngelPad, Chicago New Venture Challenge, MuckerLab, StartX, Techstars, Y Combinator.[28]

Navigating Through Growth And Constant Change

SCALING COMPANIES AND COMMUNITIES

ack in Joe's conference room, Joe was telling Liz and Rick about how Jean's company had grown from one hundred employees to two hundred in a year, and then to four hundred employees the following year. The company hit the market at just the right time, and there was an explosion of hiring and expansion in almost every area.

With growth, however, came challenges of constant change. Joe suggested they watch a short video to engage their thinking about the challenges that companies face in today's environment. With that, he pressed play on the projector. The video trumpeted on the screen:

"The top ten jobs in highest demand in 2010 did not exist in 2004…One out of eight couples married in the United States last year met online…If Facebook were a country, it would be the second largest country in the world…By 2049, a $1,000 computer will exceed the computational capacity of the entire human species…"[29]

Liz and Rick could feel their minds expanding as they listened to the video. Joe recommended they put their virtual-reality glasses back on so they could "see what rapid growth looks like." This time, they found themselves at the corporate headquarters of VT Corp., where Jean and Tom reappeared, along with someone Jean referred to as the "Builder."

In order to scale VT Corp., Jean, Dave, and VT Corp.'s board decided to hire a seasoned business builder, named Alan Chu, as COO. Alan had a background working for growth companies, and afterwards became an operating partner at a venture capital firm working with their portfolio of companies during their growth phase. Alan liked working with VT Corp. so much that he decided to join them full time.

VT Corp.'s headquarters was bustling. People were on their phones selling and serving customers. Many of the offices had people in them conducting interviews. Liz and Rick were told the company was trying to hire as fast as they could to meet growing needs, especially for software developers, sales people, and customer support.

"Liz and Rick," Jean started in, "let me introduce you to Alan. Alan is our chief operating officer. I have asked him to explain to you the difficulties we faced scaling our growing enterprise."

Jean explained that Liz and Rick were just shown a video by Joe that highlighted the significant amount of external change facing companies. She asked Alan to explain how VT Corp. was able to stay ahead of those kind of changes so that competitors didn't leapfrog them with new solutions that would have threatened their company.

Navigating across the River of Change

"The true answer is, we worried less about competition at that time and more about our own execution," said Alan. "One of our largest challenges was attracting and retaining the talent we needed to grow. The reason all our offices were full at the time is because we were interviewing like mad to keep up with our growth. Technology talent was one of the largest needs, but we also were looking for top sales, customer support, operations, and supply-chain employees as well.

"One additional challenge we faced was attracting significantly more growth capital to fund our expansion. We discovered that investors at the growth stage were different than those during the start-up stage. Unfortunately for us, we found it difficult to attract growth investors because very few were in town. As a result, it took a long time for us to develop relationships with growth investors from out of town, and we almost ran out of money again. Finally, we raised capital from an out-of-town venture capital firm in addition to Joe's firm. With their investments, we were then able to develop a relationship and line of credit with a bank that was comfortable with financing our type of growth company. The lack of growth capital in our community was a challenge that I am sure Tom will address later."

"So what were the most important things you did to prepare for, and succeed, during this growth phase?" asked Liz.

"The two most important things we did during this time were to focus on building our culture based on a collective set of values we held within our company, and also to create what we refer to as our stakeholder partner network."

Building Engaging Cultures

"In order to attract, retain, and engage the employee talent we needed to grow, we realized very quickly that we needed to work on creating a great culture, reputation, and place to work. Did you know that three hundred and fifty billion dollars are squandered each year due to lost productivity from employees who have poor relationships with their supervisors or leave their jobs due to other factors typically relating to their work environment?[30]

"It is estimated that young employees today may have between ten to fourteen jobs by the time they are thirty-eight years old. You can imagine what the loss of good employees means for morale, productivity, and ultimately how well we serve our customers.

"Although Jean and Dave had developed a great working environment based on their values, we had neither solidified our culture nor engaged the entire organization in it. We wanted to tap in to the collective wisdom of our employees, ensure they all shared our company values, and encourage them to take the actions necessary to support our success. In addition, we knew by creating an engaging culture it would help our brand and ability to engage our business partners.

"Research shows that high-engagement companies outperform their peer group by a wide margin in terms of stock price performance, as well as revenue and profit growth. Unfortunately, most companies don't do the things necessary to attract and engage employees, customers, and partners."

"So how did you create a culture to support your growth, and what were your keys to engaging your employees?" asked Liz.

"To create employee engagement, we focused on defining the purpose and mission of our company and our shared values. Our purpose is first and foremost about improving the lives of individuals through transportation safety and to benefit our cities through advanced transportation solutions.

"Our shared values also involve improving the lives of our stakeholders, including employees, customers, partners, and communities. We aspire to help our customers reduce travel costs and better serve their customers. We aspire to create a great place to work for our employees and improve their lives and households. We also aspire to be a model corporate citizen and a leader in environmental, social, and governance practices. In addition, we ask our employees at all levels, as well as our stakeholders, to help us improve and innovate in everything we do.

"We take our corporate values seriously and have attempted to institutionalize them within the company. They are a big part of our hiring, onboarding, and employee review and compensation processes. We discuss them in meetings along with our business priorities and strategy. Since one of our values is to continue to be an innovative company, we made sure that as we grew we built a culture where every employee was encouraged to be a leader and find new and innovative ways to do their jobs and improve the company."

"That is very inspiring and helpful," remarked Rick. "You also mentioned a second focus of yours during this growth phase was to engage your business partners. Can you tell us about how you did this?"

Engaging Stakeholders in Partnership Networks

"Thank you for reminding me to address this," said Alan. "To succeed and grow when faced with so much change, we had to engage not only every employee within the company but also every customer, supplier, distributer, shareholder, and community partner from outside the company. Engaging each of them to their fullest required creating an emotional connection and relationship that provided mutual value. We knew that if we did this well, there would be significant benefits to the company.

"If you think of the advantages you can create in a fast-changing world, it is important to make everyone your company touches a partner. When it comes down to it, strong relationships and business networks are some of your best sources of information, barriers against competitors, and generators of new ideas. In fact, according to studies, the most innovative companies in the world collaborate three times as much with external partners on the development of new products and services as other companies, and this leads to financial and other benefits.

"In the past, most companies aspired to delight their customers through exceptional customer service. This was and is an important thing to do. Unfortunately, because sales forces are typically incentivized and measured by the volume and size of the transactions they complete, customers and business partners are often treated as transactions rather than partners. At our company, we engage our customers as business partners so we can better understand how we can help them serve their customers. We even work with our customers to co-create new products and services.

"In terms of partnering with our community, we go well beyond typical corporate social responsibility programs, which we feel are important, though often not strategic. Instead, we have focused on improving our communities through well-defined environmental, social, and governance practices. We have incorporated these practices into the strategies and operations of our company and believe they improve our culture and competitiveness.

"One final thought about building a partner network. With advances in technology, the barriers between companies and their customers and business partners are blurring. Many companies, including ours, are building technology platforms to engage employees, customers, and partners; share information critical to success; and allow them to help us co-create better solutions. We even offer opportunities for our customers to share in the value they help to create.

"In some ways, the Apple App Store is a great example of co-creating with customers and business partners. Apple provides tools to allow their partners to build new products for their customers and to share in the revenue that is created. We believe there is a continuous cycle of innovation, entrepreneurship, growth, and evolution that occurs in our company in different areas, and we have attempted as best we can to break down silos within the company and between the company and our business partners."

"Do these practices somehow divert attention from your main business or have other negative impacts on your business results?" asked Rick.

"Quite the opposite," commented Alan. "They are some of our only real competitive advantages. We cannot rely on our technology as an advantage for very long. Our culture of engagement and partnership is our secret weapon. It has helped us create an engaging brand, which in turn has led to powerful customer and partner networks. Even when significant competitors have come on the scene, we have been able to fend them off because of our engaged employees, customers, and partners."

Turning to Tom, Rick asked, "What advantages did the community provide to support VT Corp. during this growth phase?"

Building Community Infrastructure and Networks for Growth

"Listening to Alan, it is remarkable how similar our objectives as a community were during this time. Our 'builder,' if you will, was our head of economic development. He worked on plans for growth in the community, including our needs for housing, transportation, health care, education, communications, and other infrastructure.

"We wanted our community to be highly functional and a great place for people to live and work so we could attract a steady supply of trained workers for companies like Jean's to hire. As a result, we had to make it easy for people to physically get around by building high quality public transportation. In addition, we needed to ensure there was access to high-speed communications virtually anywhere in our area if we were to compete with other communities.

"As Alan mentioned, VT Corp. needed to create a growth culture and network, and so did we," continued Tom. "We had been a slow growth and provincial town before, and there was a lot of resistance to growth and change. It took a great deal of time to pass many of the initiatives we proposed for growth, and creating a growth culture within our community was not easy. Ultimately, it took leadership from all sectors coming together to make it happen.

"Luckily we had, and still have, a strong community leadership network that helped us develop our community's growth policies and strategies. We also had good statistics, and projected that the increased number of businesses would create additional tax dollars to fund the needed infrastructure plus additional sports and arts venues that we previously had difficulty funding."

"What did you do to help create growth capital in the community, like venture capital firms?" asked Liz.

"It was difficult for us to attract venture capital firms to our community, and this has been a weakness within our ecosystem. Growth companies, like VT Corp., were still able to secure capital outside of the community, however, it was just more difficult for them and took longer. In addition, we lost the institutional knowledge that venture capital firms retain from evaluating emerging industries, technologies, and companies. Instead, we were strengthening other firms and communities by not having enough growth capital here. We knew this was not ideal, but we did not know what to do about it.

"Finally, a number of business leaders and wealthy individuals from the community expressed interest in investing in a professional venture capital firm within the community, and we were able to connect them to seasoned investors raising money to this end. We also determined that our university endowment could invest capital into a local venture capital firm, so they became an investor in another VC firm as well. This was the way our initial venture capital firms were started, and the number of firms has grown over time as more and more entrepreneurs have spun out of established companies to start their own ventures."

"Jean, Dave, and Alan were very lucky to have grown their company in this community because it had most of the resources they needed at this point in their company's history," commented Joe. "As they began to dominate their industry, however, they were faced with a whole new set of challenges, as was our community.

"This brings us to the final stage of the journey: evolution, which occurs through continuous innovation."

Insights about Growth

- High-growth companies offer a return to shareholders five times greater than medium-growth companies and are more likely to have long-term success.[31]
- There were over 159 unicorn companies, which are private companies with at least $1 billion in market value as of January 2016. A significant number are in areas that transform lives, such as life sciences, agriculture, health care, and the democratization of communications, Internet access, and financial services.[32]
- Approximately 30 percent of global corporate revenues in 2005 were a direct result of alliances, up from only 2 percent in 1980.[33]
- According to PwC's 2016 Global CEO Survey, 49 percent of global CEOs are expecting to make a strategic alliance in 2016…among the top reasons for forming alliances according to US respondents in the 18th PWC Global CEO survey were access to new and emerging technologies and strengthening innovation capabilities.[34]
- The venture capital industry in the United States in 2015 marked the second-highest full-year investment total in the last twenty years. Software was by far the largest category of investment, followed by health care and medical devices.[35]
- In 2016, the crowdfunding industry is on track to surpass the entire funding from the venture capital industry.[36]

Evolving Despite A Wall Of Resistance

CREATING ENDURING SUCCESS WITH CONTINUOUS
INNOVATION

As a new virtual image appeared, Liz, Rick, and Joe found themselves sitting in chairs against a wall surrounding a large conference room table. Jean and Tom were at their side. Jean pointed out the tall, worldly looking man in his sixties who was the current CEO of the board of VT Corp. His name was Rob Christianson, though Jean referred to him as a "market maker." Rob participated in a number of global regulatory boards and even testified before Congress on policies relating to the driverless car. He also periodically sat in on community planning board meetings, which is where they found themselves now.

Rob was talking about the wall of resistance that had grown up against VT Corp. now that it dominated their industry. With VT Corp.'s success, Rob was concerned about the amount of regulation that was being thrust on the company by local and global regulators. Rob was also worried that the pressures of being a public company were causing VT Corp. to lose its competitive edge due to short-term thinking, which was causing the company to be over-managed and squashing its innovation culture. Rob knew if VT Corp. were to stay ahead of the competition, it would need to continuously innovate, expand into new countries, and introduce new products that could move the financial needle for the company.

It was clear that the community's and VT Corp.'s priorities were starting to diverge more and more. The community was becoming increasingly concerned about the inequities that were growing in the local community, citizens being left out of the innovation economy due to a lack of Internet access and training for available jobs, and increases in the cost of living that were creating a situation where many would have to move out of the city or possibly move to a more affordable community altogether.

As a result, both VT Corp. and the community were facing an increased wall of resistance from their stakeholders in different ways, and both knew they would need to evolve to create sustainable success.

"Now that we have become highly successful," said Rob, "we are worried about staying ahead of the competition and continuing to innovate. Do you realize that the average life-span of a public company in the S&P 500 is shrinking rapidly? So no company is immune to the effects of change, and VT Corp. is no exception."

"We have already dealt with significant challenges as we have grown but are now facing renewed resistance. In the past, we saw strong barriers to the driverless car from incumbent automobile companies. They did not want to see the implementation of the driverless car occur because they felt it had negative ramifications for their businesses, potentially decreasing demand for, or even obsoleting, their existing fleet of cars. As a result, the traditional automobile companies put pressure on the government to slow down investment in the driverless car, and they spent money on ad campaigns questioning its safety.

"Then we had to deal with the automobile and taxi worker unions," continued Rob, "who were concerned that driverless cars could impact their jobs and even put taxi drivers out of business. There was no question there would be job dislocations, but our research showed that there would be an increase in high-paying tech jobs and jobs required to retool streets with sensors and new infrastructure for driverless cars.

"Today," said Rob, "we continue to work our way through these issues, however, we are worried that increased regulations could stifle our growth. We are also worried about the increase in our state and local taxes, as well as the growth in the cost of living within our community. As a result of these increased costs, we are required to raise wages, and this is hurting our profitability."

At this point, the mayor spoke up. "We are supportive of driverless car legislation, and understand how much safer it will be when we don't have to worry about others drinking, texting, or otherwise driving impaired. We also know from studies that computers in cars for the most part can make better decisions than humans. Still, there are concerns from citizens about safety and even about terrorists wreaking havoc in our streets by hacking into the transportation nerve system of the driverless car.

"In addition, the driverless car is only one of our priority initiatives as we seek to apply new technologies to improve the lives of all our citizens. We have faced, and overcome, challenges to fund and build the infrastructure to support growth in areas such as transportation, healthcare, education, communications, and housing. With our success, however, have come other challenges.

"The largest issues, and top priorities for the city now, are to ensure we maintain an affordable and livable city that retains its diversity and regional assets while evolving to sustainably support even more growth. We want to ensure that the opportunities created by the innovation economy are available to all our citizens, which we refer to as 'digital equity.'"

As the mayor continued on, Joe whispered to Liz and Rick on the side regarding his observations relating to innovation and change, and why a wall of resistance can stifle new competition.

"One thing that creates resistance to new innovation and change, which I have observed time and again, is the unintended consequences that invariably result. For instance, with the driverless car, and many other new innovations, there will be a change in the makeup of work and a requirement to develop new skills for new jobs. In addition, with all the sensors that make the driverless car work, the video cameras that protect our streets, and software that tracks the driverless car, people rightly worry about losing their privacy. In truth, they have increasingly and willingly lost their privacy a long time ago with the introduction of social media and other technology platforms, however, it will be even more pronounced in the future.

"In addition, although there is a lower risk of human accident with driverless cars and our interconnected transportation grid, cyber terrorism is an equally worrisome threat as smart cities become increasingly connected. Today, VT Corp. is constantly trying to prevent hackers from breaking into the driverless-car command center and wreaking major havoc. The same is true with hacking into the electric power grid within our community. There seems to be a never-ending stream of cyber attacks, and the only good that has come of it is an increase in jobs in the cyber security area.

"With that said, there is one consistent reality," continued Joe, "and that is you cannot stop innovation or the change it brings. You can only guide it with the policies and regulations that protect the rights of our citizens, and continue to find ways to engage people in the innovation economy as broadly as possible."

The mayor was now concluding his remarks. "These are all possible hurdles we must face, and we have taken every precaution to address them. On the positive side, there is significant support from environmental groups that see the driverless car as a way to reduce pollution and traffic congestion. Still, we have a fight on our hand and will need to educate the community in order to pass an initiative to pay for driverless-car infrastructure. At the end of the day, we are expecting it to take longer than any of us thought to work through the remaining issues. Also, as I mentioned, the driverless car is only one of the issues we will need to address if we are going to create a community that continues to be a great place to live and work."

Community Evolution

With that, the mayor introduced his head of economic development to talk about what they were doing to plan for advances not only in support of the driverless car but also to implement other policies and innovation to improve the city. The mayor knew how important it would be to create a vision of the future that the community could rally around ,and had tapped his head of economic development to take the lead in creating that vision.

The head of economic development had put together a task force to research what other communities had done to create digital equity and sustainable growth. The task force also conducted interviews with members of community-based organizations, academia, and local business leaders, as well as held community roundtable discussions to hear in more detail from the various constituents within the community.

As the head of economic development stood up and headed to the projector, he started by thanking the mayor. Then he addressed the council.

"Thank you, council members, for being here. We have spent a great deal of time studying the needs of our community as we have grown and developed our priorities. As you know, we started by creating our principles and values for digital equity within our community, which guide our decisions, investments, and program priorities."

The head of economic development turned on the projector, and up came the first slide with their guiding principles.

Guiding Principles

1. Elimination of Barriers: Eliminate structural barriers so that digital assets are available to all.
2. Strategic Focus: Link digital equity work to strategic areas, including education, jobs, health, safety, and civic engagement.
3. Cross-Sector Collaboration: Work together to provide solutions that involve government, nonprofits, academia, and business.
4. Inclusive Economic Development: Ensure that digital equity for all is part of the economic plan for all communities within our city.

"With these goals and guiding principles in mind, we are pursuing a number of priority programs," he continued.

"First, we have already helped to bring affordable Internet access to over eighty-five percent of the population in our community. We would like to further bring access to the other fifteen percent.

In addition, we are working on ways to bring higher-speed Internet access to as many people as is feasible. We know from studies that this will continue to attract new companies, provide an efficient way to work from home for a growing number of remote workers, and improve access for our citizens to information, education, entertainment, and other services.

"Second, we are making affordable devices available to everyone in need by encouraging the refurbishment of used computers and cell phones.

"Third, we are making skills training available to residents online and providing placement services for available jobs that are being created by the innovation economy.

"Finally, we are putting in place policies for affordable housing to ensure that people of all income levels, as well as families, can afford to live in our city for a long time.

"To accomplish these objectives, we have created public-private partnerships in the areas of high-speed Internet access as well as skills training. For high-speed Internet access, we are making spare fiber-optic capacity available to Internet service providers wanting to expand their service. We are also providing publicly sponsored hotspots throughout the city and working with the US Department of Housing and Urban Development to encourage broadband adoption for families with children. In addition, we are working with the private sector to develop skills training programs to meet their hiring needs.

"One of our strategic focus areas outlined in our guiding principles is education. We believe our K-12 education system needs to prepare our children to keep up with the developing needs for jobs in our innovation economy. This must start as early as possible so that our youth have the foundational knowledge and tools to succeed in the future. Our success requires good science, technology, engineering, and math education. It also requires teaching our children entrepreneurial leadership skills, and encouraging them to try them out in areas where they have passion.

"In addition, education now requires continuous learning for our existing workers whose jobs are no longer needed, are in transition, or are reaching retirement age. Given we have had many more jobs, especially in tech, than trained people to fill them, this is a top priority. We hope to greatly increase teacher capacity and tech curricula in the future to fill the gaps that exist."

At this point, a council member interrupted, "This sounds good, but how are we going to get agreement on all the changes required?"

Creating Enduring Innovation Communities

The mayor stood up to answer the question, "Well, the short answer is that it is going to take leadership from all areas to be successful. When we started the process of building our community, we had the idea that we could be an innovation center with all the elements to harness innovation and entrepreneurship for economic growth and to improve the quality of life in our community.

"We have come a long way to make that dream a reality. Today, we have a strong university system, established corporations, well-funded investment firms, and a supportive government. Many of the leaders of these institutions are sitting around this table and are supportive pillars for innovation and entrepreneurship. Through our joint efforts, we have built a collaborative start-up ecosystem and have many more entrepreneurs founding companies than ever before. In addition, we have built the infrastructure to attract companies and talent to our community. Because of these efforts, our community has grown, and we are thriving economically."

The mayor then transitioned to a call for help. "To become an enduring, healthy, and inclusive community, however, we still have much to accomplish. It is important to realize that our city does not stand on its own but is part of a global community. We can learn from other communities going through similar challenges. We can collaborate with global institutions as well. Most of all, it will take a collective effort by leaders from all areas within our community, including industry, government, education, finance, nonprofit, and intermediaries, to ensure we achieve the priorities we outlined today. I see this leadership council as critically important not only for the future health of our community but also for the long-term success of the companies headquartered here."

As the mayor finished his remarks, Rob stood up to say how appreciative he and his company were for all the community had done to support them. He pointed out that VT Corp. went through similar stages of growth and benefitted from the resources the community provided.

Creating Enduring Innovative Companies

"Just like you, we built our company on innovation first," said Rob. "Jean came up with the initial concept for the products and software based on her work at the university and car company. She then met Dave at the incubator, and he became Jean's entrepreneurial partner, which was the beginning of the start-up phase of VT Corp. Together, they raised money to launch and grow, built the initial products the company offered, and identified our initial customers. All these initial supporters and customers came from the community.

"As our company grew, Alan came on board to help formalize our processes, systems, and culture. Like you, we focused on building an engaging and innovative culture by formalizing our values and guiding principles. One of our guiding principles is to treat all our stakeholders as partners. This we believe has been critical for attracting and engaging the type of talent, resources, and customers we have needed to grow. Again, much of the human talent, financial resources, and a number of customers during our growth phase came from the community.

"Now we are global and are building our business around the world. This has involved finding global talent and continuing to attract capital from around the world. In addition, from a business perspective, we are working to ensure that we stay innovative while we attempt to meet the short-term expectations of Wall Street. We want innovation to be part of everyone's job, and to identify ways to create enduring growth. We have been successful so far, but we continue to have a sense of urgency to achieve even greater milestones.

"One of our initiatives is to create continuous innovation. To accomplish this, we have had to stay in the flow of information about our competition and new technology solutions that could disrupt our business. We have done this in part by creating a robust intelligence network with innovation outposts in major technology centers around the world, like Silicon Valley in the United States and Tel Aviv in Israel. In addition, we are lucky that our headquarters is in this community, which is an up-and-coming innovation and entrepreneurship center.

"We have used these innovation outposts to identify technology talent, incubate new ideas, invest and partner alongside top venture capitalists, and acquire promising start-ups to shorten our time to market for new products in adjacent markets. In fact, that is how we ended up acquiring the company that manufactures the virtual-reality glasses we are wearing."

"I did not know VT Corp. acquired a virtual-reality company," said Rick to Jean. "How does virtual reality fit into VT Corp.'s transportation roadmap?"

"We look at our company as an alternative to the traditional transportation industry. We initially used virtual reality in our design and manufacturing processes, which is how we were first introduced to our virtual-reality company. We then were asked by a number of our customers if we had anything that could improve the passenger experience during their commute now that there were no longer drivers. This is when we began looking at virtual reality as another product in our arsenal, selling complementary solutions to the same customer."

"Now that you are global, what role does the community continue to play for VT Corp?" asked Rick.

"This community has been instrumental to our initial founding and growth," continued Jean, "and we want to ensure it stays an affordable and livable community for our employees. One of our core values is to improve the lives of all our stakeholders, including the community, and we believe our community creates the type of resources and entrepreneurial environment we need to thrive in the future. Through this core value, we are improving lives not only within the community but for all of our stakeholders."

"So how do you see the mission of improving lives integrated into the operations of VT Corp. and our community?" asked Liz, looking at Jean and Tom.

"This is a topic I know Liz and Rick are keenly interested in," interrupted Joe, "however, Jean and Tom need to move on to other meetings. Let me suggest that we say good-bye to them and continue this discussion back in my conference room."

Insights About Innovation and Evolution

- Of 190 companies in the S&P 500 that disclosed R&D spending in 2014, the most innovative companies outperformed the overall index. They also grew at a much faster rate than other companies.[37]
- The top ten most innovative public companies in the world according to outside surveys are Apple, Google, Tesla Motors, Samsung, Amazon, GE, 3M, Microsoft, IBM, and Toyota.[38]
- A PwC Pulse survey of CEOs in North and South America, Europe, Asia Pacific, and the Middle East reveals that 97 percent of CEOs see innovation as a top priority for their businesses.[39]
- The most innovative start-up communities in the world measured by the quality of talent, pool of venture-capital resources, experience and mentorship provided by start-up founders, market reach of their companies, and the ultimate performance and exit value of their companies are Silicon Valley, New York City, Los Angeles, Boston, Tel Aviv, London, Chicago, Seattle, Berlin, and Singapore.[40]
- The top future-ready cities in the United States, according to a Harvard study and measured by how they attract and nurture human capital; foster collaborative, growth-oriented commercial environments; and build an enabling foundation of technology, telecom, and physical infrastructure, are San Jose; San Francisco; Washington, DC; Boston; Austin; Raleigh; Seattle; Denver; Portland; Dallas–Fort Worth; New York; Minneapolis–Saint Paul; Houston; Atlanta; Charlotte; San Diego; Chicago; Louisville; Salt Lake City; Des Moines; Los Angeles; Pittsburgh; Kansas City; Columbus; and Philadelphia.[41]

Transforming Lives In The Innovation Economy

THE CHALLENGES AND OPPORTUNITIES IMPACTING THE WAY WE WORK AND LIVE

Rick and Liz took off their virtual-reality headsets, and were face-to-face with Joe in his conference room. Joe started the discussion about transforming lives through innovation and entrepreneurship by saying:

"As we start the discussion about the mission and purpose of companies, and how they can transform lives, I do not want to lose an important point, which is that there is no platform for doing good without a sound financial business that makes money. It is an absolute requirement. Great leaders build financially strong companies and find the right balance along the spectrum of doing well financially and good for their stakeholders. This is a difficult task, however, there is no enduring ability to do good without enduring profits."

"With that said," continued Joe, "one way to think about how inventions, companies, and communities improve lives is by looking at the innovation, economic, and societal value they create. I brought a handout that describes these various areas of value and the way I think of them."

With that, Joe handed out a piece of paper with the following table on it.

	Innovation Value	Economic Value	Societal Value
Life-Enhancing Inventions	New knowledge and intellectual property	New companies, employment, licensing, and network extensions	Life-enhancing discoveries, companies, and nonprofits
Enduring Innovation Companies	Innovative products, practices, and cultures that sustain companies	Employment growth, sale of goods and services, and network extensions	Improvement in the lives of stakeholder-partners wherever they reside
Enduring Innovation Communities	Community ecosystem supporting innovation and start-up companies	Growth in inventions, companies, employment, tax dollars, and network extensions	Improvement in the lives of citizens within the community and shared knowledge globally

"Let me explain this table to you. Let's start by reviewing the value that inventions create, which is vast."

Life-Enhancing Inventions

McKinsey, a top management consulting firm, outlined in a paper the technologies that will transform life, business, and the global economy. It forecasted significant benefits in areas such as (1) advanced robotics, which is being used in 250 million annual surgeries; (2) next-generation genomics in medicine, benefiting 26 million people who die annually from cancer, cardiovascular disease, and type 2 diabetes, and in agriculture, impacting 2.5 billion people; (3) energy storage, impacting 1.2 billion people without access to electricity, and (4) the mobile Internet, connecting 4.3 billion people who are without Internet access in the world, among other transformative innovations.[42]

"Inventions create knowledge and intellectual property that can lead to economic value, such as licensing revenue, new companies, and new employment. Additionally, the value created extends to the network of professionals that helps commercialize these technologies, such as licensing and patent attorneys, financial professionals, and others.

"In terms of social value, new discoveries can lead to products, services, companies, and nonprofits that enhance life by improving our health, food, housing, environment, transportation, communications, and in many others areas."

Enduring Innovation Companies

"Turning to enduring innovation companies, they are the ones with innovative and purpose-driven cultures, practices, and solutions that allow them to constantly evolve and grow. Along with growth, they create new employment as well as goods and services.

"The economic value created by enduring innovation companies extends to their network of stakeholder partners, including customers, distributors, suppliers, shareholders, and communities. These partners all grow with, and in support of, enduring companies. In addition, the network extensions include professional advisers and other intermediaries who are contracted to advise or provide services to these companies.

"In terms of social value, enduring companies find ways to engage and improve the lives of their stakeholders. Employees are treated as partners, receive ongoing education, and reap the benefits of fair compensation, benefits, and, in some cases, ownership. This in turn leads to more engaged and committed employees.

"In addition, customers, distributors, and suppliers are also treated as partners receiving information, training, tools, research, and other benefits that allow them to co-create better solutions and mutually beneficial business models. Finally, enduring companies engage in their communities strategically and for mutual benefit, identifying ways to incorporate community partners and activities into the strategies and operations of the company. This again leads to mutually beneficial relationships and competitive advantages over time."

Enduring Innovation Communities

"Enduring innovation communities are those that constantly evolve and grow by creating policies, practices, and cultures that attract innovators, entrepreneurs, and investors and lead to robust innovation and entrepreneurship ecosystems.

"These communities in turn develop economic benefits, including new knowledge, inventions, companies, employment, and tax dollars for their communities. In addition, as these communities grow, they develop networks of real estate developers, nonprofits, and support organizations, that also benefit.

"Enduring innovation communities also invest in technologies and infrastructure required to continuously attract talent and resources to the community. They retain their regional identities, are inclusive and equitable, and remain affordable and livable. This is a difficult task, and innovation centers that have grown quickly have found it very hard to accomplish these goals.

"Now that I have outlined this framework, let me ask how it fits with what you, Liz and Rick, learned from the people you met during the innovation journey."

Lessons Learned about Transforming Lives

Liz started by discussing what she had learned about enduring innovation companies that transform lives. "The greatest lesson I learned about enduring innovation companies is that they all have the potential to transform lives through the way they are led, treat their employees, and serve their customers and communities. It comes down to the values of the founders and leaders to shape a culture that is dedicated to doing well financially and doing good for its stakeholder partners.

"It is also interesting to me," continued Liz, "to learn that companies can be much more strategic about how they engage their employees to advance the goals of their companies and the communities they serve. I always thought that companies gave back to communities out of responsibility and to engage their employees in volunteer activities as good corporate citizens through their corporate social responsibility programs. It seems, however, that there are ways to engage in improving communities that improve the capabilities and value of companies as well.

"In terms of innovation companies that transform lives, Jean taught me the importance of clearly defining problems in order to come up with solutions. When there are large societal problems, such as finding better transportation solutions, there can oftentimes be profitable business opportunities as well.

"Alan taught me the importance of creating engaging cultures and business partner networks, and how this can lead to accelerated innovation, adaptability, and competitiveness through the co-creation of solutions built on technology platforms. For VT Corp., their business-partner network extends to the communities they serve and is one of their core values.

"Finally, Rob provided great insights as to why new innovation is resisted and how important it is for highly successful and mature corporations like VT Corp. to collaborate with leaders from other sectors to build communities that attract talent and resources, which are good for the community and for business. VT Corp., because of its values, also was able to incorporate environmental, social, and governance practices into their operations, such as aspiring to achieve zero carbon emissions and transparency wherever possible in the information they provide. They have not only talked about this but also have funded initiatives to accomplish and measure progress toward these goals."

Turning to Rick, Joe asked what he had learned about building enduring communities that transform lives.

"The first thing I learned," said Rick, "is communities that foster innovation and entrepreneurship are the most likely to grow and be relevant in the future, and those without an innovation foundation are likely to become less competitive over time.

"Second, I learned that enduring communities built on innovation and entrepreneurship require a number of key anchor institutions to be engaged and collaborative in order to tackle the many challenges that occur through the various stages. In addition, they require government leaders to put in place the policies, investment priorities, and culture, that allow innovation and growth to more readily occur.

"Finally, from the community leadership council meeting we attended it is clear that enduring innovation communities need strong cross-sector community leadership to support a healthy and inclusive community. At the council meeting, there appeared to be the will to share the benefits of an innovation community as broadly as possible, retain the unique elements that make the community great, and provide the opportunity for as many people as possible to participate in the innovation economy."

Rick then turned the tables on Joe and asked, "We have talked about the pluses and minuses of innovation, and I wonder whether you see innovation as a net positive or negative?"

Joe had clearly thought deeply about this question.

The Challenges and Opportunities of Innovation

"Rick, I am an optimist, and I believe most people will use technology for good. I see innovation companies in industries such as healthcare, energy, and education that have the opportunity to transform entire industries and directly improve lives.

"I see rising investor interest in impact and socially responsible investing, with trillions of dollars being committed to companies with strong environmental, social, and governance leadership because those companies have the potential to transform lives *and* achieve competitive financial returns.

"With that said, I am also a pragmatist and know we need to always keep a watchful eye out for those who wish to use technology for counterproductive ends. Technology can be used for good, but without proper controls and regulation, it can be exploited for evil. It can be overused as well, and people can miss out on the relationships and natural beauty that is around us.

"In addition, the innovation economy can contribute to the growing digital divide and wealth inequities that come from either being part of, or excluded from, it. There is also a great deal of worry about workers being displaced by machines and artificial intelligence, which could lead to significant dislocations.

"With that said, I believe with great leadership, and the will, more people will participate in the economic benefits of this new world economy. So I am very hopeful.

"Now, with the remaining time we have left, I would like to switch to one final topic, which you both asked me about," said Joe, "and that is what job opportunities exist, and what it will take to prepare for them, in the innovation economy."

Insights about Transforming Lives in the Innovation Economy

- The president's Council of Economic Advisers under President Obama estimates that if the United States had maintained the rapid pace of post–World War II productivity growth from the 1970s till today, the average American household would have an additional $30,000 in income.[43]
- The Internet Association reports the Internet's economic impact doubled from 2007 to 2014, nearing three million total jobs. The Internet sector was responsible for an estimated $966.2 billion, or 6 percent, of real gross domestic product in 2014.[44]
- *Fortune*'s ranking of the top companies changing the world according to the degree of business innovation involved, the measurable impact at scale on an important social challenge, the contribution of the shared-value activities to the company's profitability and competitive advantage, and the significance of the shared value effort to the overall business include Vodafone, Google, Toyota, Walmart, Enel, GSK, Jain Irrigation Systems, Cisco Systems, Novartis, and Facebook.[45]
- In the United States, seventy-five IP-intensive industries employ forty million workers, create $5.0 trillion in value, and represent 35.5 percent of US gross domestic product.[46] For every computer-science job created, between five and seven other jobs are created as well.[47]
- A study of 120 nations between 1980 and 2006 estimated that each ten-point increase in broadband penetration adds 1.3 percent to a high-income country's gross domestic product and 1.21 percent for low- to middle-income nations.[48]
- Jim Collins, in his book *Built to Last*, concluded that purpose- and values-driven organizations outperformed the general market by 15:1.[49] In a second study lasting over an eleven-year period and published by Harvard professors John Kotter

and Jim Heskett, it was found that firms with cultures that emphasized all the key managerial constituencies and leadership from managers at all levels outperformed firms that did not have those traits by a wide margin.[50]

Engaging In The Innovation Economy—Are You Ready?

PREPARING YOURSELF FOR THE OPPORTUNITIES IN THE
INNOVATION ECONOMY

J oe turned on the projector so that he could display a diagram that he felt would help frame the discussion about the job opportunities within the innovation economy.

"Now that we have discussed the stages of the innovation journey, let's talk about the changing workforce landscape. As a backdrop, not only is the makeup of the workforce changing, but so is the way people collaborate and work. For instance, Liz, your generation of millennials is now the largest group of workers and growing. They are demanding more flexibility to work virtually anywhere and to have more work-life balance. At the same time, Rick, your generation of baby boomers is rapidly retiring from full-time employment. They desire more part-time work than ever before.

"In addition, the nature of work is changing with lower level jobs being replaced by robots, and other jobs being replaced by machine learning. There is a need for different types of workers with new skill sets, and individuals committed to life-long learning to keep up with the rapid rate of change.

"Separately, companies are no longer islands that stand alone with their employees on one island and customers, suppliers, distributors, and other partners on their own separate islands. Instead, more and more bridges are being built between all of these stakeholders, and technology is helping to enable online communities and networks that allow for much greater collaboration. The same is true with physical communities, which do not stand alone but are increasingly part of regional, national, and global networks and economies.

"With that said, let me explain the innovation employment flywheel diagram displayed here so we can organize our discussion around employment opportunities at various stages. I call this diagram a flywheel because when trained talent is readily available to fill the opportunities in the innovation economy, then it starts a wheel moving that leads to ongoing growth in companies, jobs, and prosperity.

"First, let's discuss the spokes of the flywheel. These are the types of organizations where innovation and entrepreneurship opportunities exist. As you can see, these include opportunities in corporations, including start-ups and enduring companies, that you are interested in, Liz. In addition, there are opportunities in government, nonprofits, universities, and other educational institutions; intermediaries, such as professional advisers and associations; and investment firms, which are all areas you may be interested in, Rick."

INNOVATION ECONOMY FLYWHEEL

Employment Opportunities in the Innovation Economy

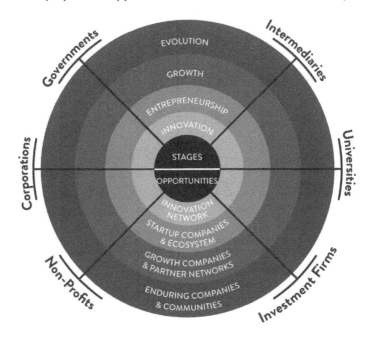

"The top half of the diagram outlines the stages of the innovation journey, including the innovation, entrepreneurship (start-up), growth, and evolution stages. The bottom half of the diagram outlines the companies, networks, and ecosystems that correspond to the various stages above. At each stage, companies have different ways they operate that may or may not be a fit with someone's skills and interests. In addition, at each stage, company and community networks and ecosystems provide opportunities for employment and engagement. Let me outline the opportunities at each stage of the journey. Liz and Rick, you can decide which opportunities are most appealing to you."

Innovation Stage Opportunities

"If you are interested in innovation stage opportunities, then it is oftentimes critical that you develop a high degree of technical and industry expertise. With deep expertise in an area, there are opportunities for researchers, lab workers, and inventors. The physical space you will likely work in is a maker space, such as a lab environment or machine shop, that has the equipment to support researchers and inventors.

"In terms of the networks, some help advance knowledge in the field connecting inventors with each other and other experts. Other networks assist with commercialization efforts, and create opportunities for grant writers helping to attract government or foundation funding, patent attorneys helping to formalize the intellectual property that is created, and licensing agents selling intellectual property to corporate and government customers. There are also investment firms and incubators that specialize in funding inventors from universities and national labs, and helping them to spin out companies based on their inventions.

"The community institutions and ecosystems at the innovation stage include government and foundation funders, research universities, corporate R&D centers, plus a number of local, regional, and national nonprofits and associations."

Entrepreneurship (Start-Up) Stage Opportunities

"Another set of opportunities relate to start-up companies. If this stage appeals to you, then you will need to be comfortable working in an environment with a lack of structure, a lot of ambiguity and risk, and a lack of mentorship from leaders who are too busy 'doing' to spend time mentoring. On the other hand, if you like to jump in and help shape an organization from the beginning, there are no better companies to work for.

"As we have discussed in the past, there are also opportunities to help start-up companies as part of a founding group that includes investors, advisers who sit on boards and advisory boards, and key legal and financial professionals who support the corporate and fundraising requirements at this stage.

"The nice thing about advising companies during the start-up stage," continued Joe, "is that most of them are local, and you can have personal interactions with the founders. On the other hand, if you are part of a founding group, you also need to be comfortable with a great deal of ambiguity and failure as well as the willingness to help the founders raise rounds of funding.

"During this stage there are also opportunities to work within start-up community ecosystems that consist of institutions that support start-up companies. They include incubators; accelerators; professional legal, financial, human resources, recruiting, and other advisers who specialize in start-ups; seed investors from angel networks, venture capital firms, and private family offices; university innovation and entrepreneurship programs and tech transfer offices; as well as associations supporting start-ups. There are also government-sponsored programs and city planners that work with real-estate developers to build clusters of office spaces to house start-up companies and allow for easy collaboration between entrepreneurs and their support networks. These are often referred to as 'innovation districts.'"

Growth Stage Opportunities

"As companies grow, they have a very different feel and needs for talent than start-ups. In growth companies, there is constant activity, as we saw when we met Alan, with way too much for any individual to accomplish. Growth companies require leaders and employees at all levels to prioritize initiatives and their own work activities. Similar to start-ups, there is often little time for mentoring, and individuals must learn as they go.

"On the other hand, there is more structure typically with growth companies than start-ups, and there is the opportunity to choose between functional areas such as sales, marketing, finance, and product management. In addition, you will find job opportunities are plentiful for employees with the right skills or even for 'raw athletes' willing to learn in growth companies. In addition, there are frequent opportunities to take on additional work and for career advancement.

"The networks surrounding growth companies also create significant opportunities. They include growth investors; seasoned board members; a broad group of professional advisers and consultants, such as investment bankers and deal lawyers, looking to help with acquisitions; recruiters helping to identify essential talent to grow; and human-resource experts that help put in place plans, policies, and processes for hiring, compensating, firing, and complying with labor laws.

"There are also opportunities for functional advisers, consultants, and outsourcing experts to support areas such as sales, customer support, technology, operations, investor relations, supply chains, distribution, and other functional areas. In addition, as companies grow and expand geographically and within industry sectors, they often seek help from those with geographic and industry expertise.

"Growth companies look to the community to support their growth by investing in infrastructure in all areas, from housing, health care, education, transportation, communications, and energy, to parks and recreation. By doing so, companies can more easily attract the talent they need to grow, and it is easier to conduct business.

"As cities focus on planning and implementing infrastructure for growth, there are opportunities for individuals to participate on committees in all the areas mentioned previously. There are also opportunities to work with nonprofit groups that support infrastructure growth and healthy communities. Typically, state universities also have programs in many of these areas with opportunities to volunteer. For instance, Jean, in addition to her company duties, sits on a number of committees and nonprofit boards relating to transportation, which helps the community and helps her with connections that are valuable for her company."

Evolution Stage Opportunities

"As companies become global leaders in their industry, and communities are successful in becoming enduring innovation centers, there are even more opportunities that arise.

"Large corporations can be stable places to work with significant opportunities for training and mentorship. On the other hand, many corporations have not been successful in retaining their innovation culture but instead have become beholden to Wall Street and quarterly earnings. Many of these corporations have execution cultures that can be quite stifling, and oftentimes there is not as much control and stability for employees as there once was.

"As companies build global operations, they frequently need help understanding how best to operate in different countries with distinct cultures. These companies also have diverse workforces because of their global footprint, and they must become increasingly effective at supporting diversity within their companies. In addition, they need sophisticated accounting and control systems, communications infra-structure, and other systems that allow them to operate effectively on a global basis. Finally, category-leading companies often look at acqui-sitions as a way to support growth in adjacent areas and geographies. In support of these and other needs of global companies, there are full- and part-time opportunities for individuals with the appropriate expertise in these areas.

"As for communities that have achieved success and grown sig-nificantly, they are dealing with different needs than at previous stages. Most enduring communities are tackling issues such as afford-ability, livability, inclusiveness, and equity. Again, there are ways to get involved with government agencies, nonprofits, associations, and universities focusing on initiatives in all these areas. In addition, there are frequently cross-sector leadership councils like the one we sat in on with Rob that provide opportunities to participate on task forces."

Joe paused at this point to ask Liz and Rick where their inter-ests lie on the innovation economy flywheel, and what their current thinking is about the job opportunities that might be appealing to them.

"This overview helps confirm that there are many, many oppor-tunities to participate in the innovation economy from a business and community perspective," said Liz. "Given my interest in business and entrepreneurship, it is clear that I have a lot to learn about leading a company through the various stages. In some ways, it was better not knowing all of this because, beforehand, it did not seem so daunting. On the other hand, I read that many entrepreneurs work in existing businesses awhile before starting their companies, which is the way I am leaning. So I would ideally look for a growth company for which to work.

"Also, from an entrepreneur's perspective, I now realize how important it is to develop my personal network, and it will become a high priority of mine. There are many people and resources I can tap in to at our university and within our community, especially within our start-up hubs, incubators, and accelerators, as well as professional advisers who will be critical to my success when I am ready to start my own company. I plan to spend time learning about these networks now and attending a number of events to develop my relationships."

"From my perspective," added Rick, "I see a lot of opportunities to support entrepreneurial businesses as well as our community. I could very easily see myself as a mentor, board member, or adviser to entrepreneurs. In addition, it could be rewarding to participate as an investor with others as part of an angel network, or even support venture capitalists in town with their portfolio companies when they need operational help.

"From a community perspective, I see lots of opportunities to support innovation and entrepreneurship by sitting on boards or participating in committees at various levels within academia, government, associations, and nonprofits. There are even opportunities to connect our community with other global communities, and my background in international business has allowed me to build relationships around the world that I believe would be of value. As an aside, this would also allow my wife and me to travel more, which is a goal of ours at this point in our lives.

"As far as how to get started," continued Rick, I feel the best way is to speak with venture capitalists, angels, leaders within our state university's tech transfer office, and others to start to learn more about the opportunities that exist. This will help me build my network and uncover the types of opportunities and institutions to which I most gravitate.

Again turning the table on Joe, Rick asked: "By the way, Joe, how do you feel we best prepare ourselves to understand the opportunities that are out there?"

Preparing Yourself for Opportunities in the Innovation Economy

"There are three things I recommend and believe will be helpful, which are based in part on the work of Simon Sinek, called *Starting with Why.* Simon suggests you outline your 'why' or personal purpose statement first so you are grounded in work that will be meaningful to you. Write down your internal motivations for work, and what you want to accomplish with your life at this stage. Many people start by focusing on what they are going to do before answering the 'why' question. The 'why' answers can act as your North Star, from which you can evaluate opportunities.

"Next I would focus on your 'what,' which starts to solidify the criteria you will use to analyze opportunities. What does your perfect job look like? What stage do you feel would best fit your objectives? What size company or institution? What industry or geographic focus? What problems do you want to solve? What do you want to learn, and what organization will afford you the best opportunity to learn in those areas? What kind of culture do you want to work in? Do you want full- or part-time work? These are the types of questions that will then allow you to narrow your search.

"Finally, I would focus on the 'how' or plan of action. How can you network into the opportunities that are of most interest to you? What informational gatherings, conferences, or other meetings should you attend? How can you use tools such as LinkedIn, or recruiters or other resources to help with your search?"

Rick asked if there was any background material to read or classes to take to prepare for the discussions he was planning to have with people within his network.

"Well, there is a lot of lingo associated with any company or community organization. I have tried to capture some of the most important ones in a glossary of frequently used innovation and technology terms, which I will provide to you. (See Appendix I.)

It is more important for Liz to understand technical lingo if she is going to work for a tech company as a full-time employee, but since neither of you is going to be actively developing products, it is less important that you know details about specific technologies. Instead, I would read trade journals and go to conferences where you can learn about the technologies and companies that are gaining traction, and innovation trends that are impacting the way we live and work today.

"Of course, if you are interested in a marketing job in the technology industry, it would be important to understand the lingo and something about online marketing, search-engine optimization, and building online communities. Many community colleges and online education sites offer this kind of background. The same is true of other functional jobs within the tech industry.

"Just as important, however, is to do your homework on the companies, institutions, and individuals you plan to meet with so you have some sense of how you can add value to them. This may be obvious, but before meeting with a company or community institution, I would go to their website and research the institution, company, solutions, and competitors, as well as their key management, investors, and partners. In addition, I would go to, say, LinkedIn to understand the background of whomever you are going to speak with to see what connections you may have. For instance, did you go to the same college? Are you interested in the same activities?

"Finally, one other thing that you might find useful is to have someone, or a small group, hold you accountable and act as a sounding board as you start to narrow your search."

At this point, Liz turned to Rick and asked whether he would consider being her sounding board and mentor. "There is a lot I can learn from you and your experience, and you know a great deal about me from this journey."

Rick nodded and said, "It would be my pleasure, and I know I will learn a lot from you as well."

Joe, as always, had the final word: "Rick and Liz, it has been a pleasure spending time with both of you and guiding you on the innovation journey. It is clear that if both of you, or more broadly your generations, work together you can support one another, build enduring companies, and make meaningful, positive change in the world!"

And so began a new chapter for Liz and Rick...

Insights about Opportunities in the Innovation Economy

- In 2016, eleven of the top twenty-five highest-paying jobs are tech and engineering jobs with an average annual compensation of $96,370.[51]
- The ten best jobs based on expected growth over the next decade and pay include: app developers, nurse practitioners, information security analysts, computer systems analysts, physical therapists, market research analysts, medical sonographers, dental hygienists, operations research analysts, and health services manager.[52]
- The most digitized industries have posted the fastest wage growth, and make up about nineteen percent of total US employment.[53] Seventy-eight percent of employees believe it is important to work for a digitally enabled company or a digital leader.[54]
- Carl Benedikt Frey and Michael Osborne from Oxford Martin School estimate that the growing sophistication of artificial intelligence and robotics means that 47 percent of job roles currently available in the United States will be computerized by 2025.[55]
- By 2020, half of all workers in the United States will be freelance.[56]
- Seventy-three percent of CEOs believe that the lack of workers with key technical skills is a threat to their growth.[57]
- Fifty percent of US jobs lost in the 2008 recession were middle-skill jobs; however, only 2 percent of jobs added since 2008 are middle-skill jobs.[58]
- Goods-producing jobs have been declining for decades and now represent only 14 percent of all US jobs.[59]
- People are increasingly creating supplemental incomes from online platforms such as Airbnb, Etsy, Thumbtack, Uber, and Upwork.[60]

- Over the medium to long term, if displaced workers acquire the capabilities and training they need for new roles, the overall productivity of the US labor force could increase. The common thread running through all these changes is that skills and continuous learning matter more than ever.[61]

Postscript

The scenarios depicted herein are playing out all around the country. The United States has become a great economic power because of its ability to innovate, and enable entrepreneurs to grow companies based on their creativity, drive, and ingenuity. Our laws and culture allow for the free flow of talent and money to game-changing inventions. We celebrate the entrepreneurial spirit and closely guard the American dream. We believe that the rewards of our capitalist society should be available to anyone with the creativity, determination, and hard work to pursue them. Although we clearly have not achieved this objective yet, the United States is the leading innovation economy in the world, and a model that other countries wish to emulate.

The United States, however, cannot take its innovation excellence for granted, as globalization has rapidly enabled other countries to catch up and in some areas even surpass the United States. A Gallup study based on Census Bureau data, ranked the United States twelfth in 2015 among developed nations in terms of business start-up activity per capita. Even more alarming is that business start-ups have been declining steadily in the United States over the past thirty years, and now annual business deaths outnumber starts.[62]

In order to reverse this trend, and retain our competitive innovation advantage in the world, we will need more people trained and ready to participate in the innovation economy; additional investments in education, new innovation, and entrepreneurship; and the will to include as many individuals as possible in the innovation economy.

This mandate, if you will, is only becoming greater as innovation is speeding up the rate of change and greatly altering the way we work and live. For some, this is a scary proposition. For others, willing to embrace the challenges and opportunities that innovation brings, it is a very exciting time. If you would like to be part of the changes that are inevitably occurring, this is an invitation to come aboard and join the exciting opportunities that await you within the innovation economy. Get started on your own innovation journey so you can be counted as one who claims "iInnovate" and have changed the world for the better.

Appendix I

GLOSSARY OF FREQUENTLY USED INNOVATION TERMS

The terms in this glossary have been selected primarily to help clarify ideas in the book and are in no way an attempt to be a comprehensive glossary of all innovation and technology terms. Some of the terms are new as well.

For instance, it was hard to find a definition of the innovation economy, which is separate and distinct from the digital economy. The most closely related definition relates to "innovation capital" as defined by McKinsey & Co. In addition, the "wall of resistance" is a new term that attempts to capture what happens when a new company disrupts an existing industry. Other terms used include "enduring companies" and "enduring communities." These are distinct from "sustainable companies and communities" that emphasize environmental and other sustainability elements.

Finally, in a field laden with jargon, this glossary is an attempt to describe in plain English many of the most common terms used in the innovation economy. Many of the descriptions that follow come from Gartner Group, a technology research and consulting firm[63]; *PC Magazine*'s encyclopedia[64]; Techopedia[65]; Wikipedia[66]; the *Financial Times* Lexicon[67]; and Investopedia[68]. Other terms that are used are footnoted separately.

GLOSSARY OF TERMS

Accelerators are organizations that help entrepreneurs develop their business plans and pitches to investors over a three- to four-month time frame working with cohort groups of ten to twelve people. Accelerators also offer mentorship and education, culminating in a public investor pitch or demo day event. The first seed accelerator was Y Combinator, started in Cambridge, Massachusetts, in 2005 and later moved to Silicon Valley by Paul Graham. It was followed by TechStars in 2006.

Angel investors are individuals who invest their own money into start-up companies. Angel investors are not banks, venture capital firms, or other financial institutions, although they may invest through their family offices or as part of angel networks.

Artificial intelligence (AI) is technology that appears to emulate human performance. AI involves machines that learn, come to their own conclusions, appear to understand complex content, engage in natural dialogs with people, enhance human cognitive performance, or replace people on the execution of non-routine tasks. AI is used to detect novel concepts and abstractions and aid humans to quickly understand very large bodies of ever-changing information.

Baby boomer is the generation born between 1946 and 1964. There are seventy-six million baby boomers and, according to demographic data, by 2029 all the baby boomers will be sixty-five years or older.

Big data is information processing that enables enhanced insight, decision making, and process automation for very large amounts of data.

Blogs are websites where individuals and institutions can write about subjects of interest, express opinions, provide insights, and share information about events. Blogs also allow others to respond with their reactions, which are tracked in chronological order with the most recent entries showing up first.

Broadband is often used interchangeably with "high-speed Internet".

Cloud computing is a shared pool of technology resources (e.g., networks, servers, storage, applications, and services) maintained by a third party and "rented on demand" by individuals and organizations.

Corporate social responsibility (CSR) is a company's policies and practices relating to the impact of their businesses. CSR is also referred to as "corporate citizenship" and most often includes employee volunteer programs, corporate giving and employee matching gifts, and environmental sustainability initiatives.

Digital divide refers to the difference between people who have easy access to the Internet and those who do not. A lack of access is believed to be a disadvantage because of the huge amount of information that can only be found online. The digital divide appears in a number of different contexts including:

- differences between rural and urban Internet access;
- socioeconomic differences between people of different races, income, and education affecting their ability to access the Internet; and
- differences between developed, developing, and emerging nations in terms of the availability of Internet.

Digital economy refers to an economy that is based on digital computing technologies. The digital economy is also referred to as the Internet economy, the new economy, or the web economy. The term "digital economy" was coined in Don Tapscott's 1995 best-seller *The Digital Economy: Promise and Peril in the Age of Networked Intelligence.*[69]

Digital equity is defined as equal access to digital tools, resources, and services to increase digital knowledge, awareness, skills, and opportunities. Digital equity initiatives within communities attempt to close the digital divide as described previously.

Digital transformation describes the changes associated with the application and integration of digital technology into all aspects of human life and society. In addition, it is most often associated in the business world with companies that are striving to keep up with changing business environments brought about by new technologies.

Disruptive innovation is innovation that creates a new market and value network and eventually disrupts an existing market and value network. Digital disruption leads to the displacement of established market leaders and alliances. The term was defined by Clayton M. Christensen in 1995.

Ecosystems are groups of individuals and organizations that form an interrelated value network, such as an innovation network of investors, inventors, and academics, within a community or communities that support the development and commercialization of new ideas and technologies.

Enduring innovation communities is a new term describing communities that constantly evolve; support innovation and entrepreneurship through their policies, practices, and ecosystems; and promote diversity and social equity.

Enduring innovation companies is a new term describing companies that constantly evolve as a result of innovative cultures and practices, partnership networks, and purpose-driven leadership.

Entrepreneurship is the process of designing, launching, and running a new business, or expanding an existing one, based on new products, processes, or services. It has also been defined as the capacity and willingness to develop, organize, and manage a business venture along with any of its risks in order to make a profit.

Environmental, social, and governance (ESG) are company policies and practices that include sustainable, ethical, and corporate governance activities. ESG measures are increasingly being used by investment firms and impact investors to describe nonfinancial measures that impact a company's financial and social performance.

Impact investing refers to investments made into companies, organizations, and funds with the intention to generate a measurable, beneficial social or environmental impact alongside a financial return. Impact investing differs from socially responsible investing, which traditionally avoids investments that are inconsistent with the values of the investors, such as tobacco and arms, or companies with poor labor practices.

Incubators provide start-up companies with services, including financing, management expertise, office services, and office space. Many Internet incubators arose in the late 1990s with the intention of creating more dot-com success stories.

Innovation is described as something original and more effective and, as a consequence, new that "breaks into" the market or society. It also refers to the application of better solutions that meet new requirements, unarticulated needs, or existing market needs through more effective products, processes, services, technologies, or business models.

Innovation and entrepreneurship communities (also referred to as tech hubs, start-up cities, and future-ready cities) are urban areas with the following characteristics as described by the consulting firm BCG: (1) the ability to build, attract, and retain the world's leading innovation and entrepreneurship talent, as measured by demographics, the quality of STEM education, livability, social health, and natural environment; (2) places where business can thrive as measured by economic health, business processes, and cost of doing business; (3) capital and innovation ecosystems that provide access to capital and generate new intellectual property; (4) global connectedness and presence as measured by the movement of goods and people and their global business influence; and (5) quality of physical, transportation, and communications infrastructure.[70]

Innovation capital, as described in a report published by the consulting firm McKinsey & Company, is the value of innovation-related assets that contribute to productivity growth in the economy. Innovation capital has three components: physical capital, knowledge capital, and human capital. Physical capital is formed by investments in information and communication equipment. Knowledge capital is formed by investments that build intellectual property and brand equity, including investments in computerized information, R&D, and marketing investments as well as relevant research in universities. Human capital is formed by investments in building individual or organizational skills that drive productivity growth. This includes public and private investments in tertiary STEM education, employee-based training programs, and investments to develop organizational efficiencies (e.g., redesign of business processes or review of business models more broadly).[71]

Innovation districts are dedicating zones in cities exclusively for the purpose of clustering entrepreneurs, start-ups, business accelerators, and incubators. These spaces are easily accessible via public transportation, wired for public Wi-Fi, support mixed-use development, and nurture collaboration and knowledge sharing. The first official innovation districts were in Barcelona, Spain, with 22@, and in Boston, Massachusetts, with the Seaport Innovation District.[72]

Innovation economy describes the total economic and social value created by investments in innovation. This includes economic and social value created by new products, services, processes, companies, nonprofits, and communities, and within innovation, entrepreneurship, growth, and evolution networks. (This is distinct from the digital economy, although it subsumes it.)

Innovation hubs, as defined in Stanford's *Social Innovation Review*, contain one or more of the following elements: (1) build collaborative communities with entrepreneurial individuals at the center; (2) attract diverse members with heterogeneous knowledge, welcoming diversity in a broad sense (gender, class, and ethnicity); (3) facilitate creativity and collaboration in physical and digital space; and (4) localize global entrepreneurial culture.[73]

Intellectual property (IP) refers to inventions, ideas, and creations, that can be protected by patents, trademarks, and copyrights. According to the World Intellectual Property Organization (WIPO), there are two categories of IP: (1) industrial property that includes patents, trademarks, and industrial designs; and (2) copyrights, which refers to musical, literary, and artistic works such as songs and photographs.

Internet of Things (IoT) is the network of physical objects—devices, vehicles, buildings, and other items—embedded with electronics, software, sensors, and network connectivity that enables these objects to collect and exchange data. The IoT allows objects to be sensed and controlled remotely across existing network infrastructure, enabling smart grids, smart homes, intelligent transportation, and smart cities, among other applications.

Machine learning is a body of technology that allows computers to handle new situations via analysis, self-training, observation, and experience. Machine learning facilitates the continuous advancement of computing through exposure to new scenarios, testing, and adaptation.

Maker space (also referred to as a hackerspace) is a community-operated workspace where people with common interests, often in computers, machining, technology, science, digital art, or electronic art, can meet, socialize, and collaborate. They can be viewed as open community labs incorporating elements of machine shops, workshops, and studios where hackers can come together to share resources and knowledge to build and make things.

Millennials refers to the generation born between 1980 and 1995. There are sixty million millennials, and they today make up the largest share of the labor market.

Minimal viable product is the most pared down version of a product that can still be released. A minimal viable product has three key characteristics:

- It creates enough value that people are willing to use it or buy it initially.
- It demonstrates enough future benefit to retain early adopters.
- It provides a feedback loop to guide future development.

This concept has been popularized by Eric Ries, a consultant and writer on start-ups.

Pivoting, when used in relation to entrepreneurship, refers to a shift in strategy most often by start-ups seeking to identify the right product-market fit.[74]

Platform businesses are businesses that connect companies, customers, and partners leading to positive network effects between them. They also allow third parties to provide content or build solutions that enhance value for the platform company, third party, and customers. Examples of platform businesses include Uber, Facebook, Amazon, and Apple, among others. [75],[76]

Search-engine optimization (SEO) is used in online marketing and refers to methods used to increase traffic to a website by increasing its search-engine page rank. As an Internet marketing strategy, SEO considers how search engines work, what people search for (the actual search terms or keywords typed into search engines), and which search engines are preferred by their targeted audience.

Smart cities are designations given to cities that incorporate information and communication technologies (ICT) to enhance the quality and performance of urban services, such as energy, transportation, and utilities, in order to reduce resource consumption, waste, and overall costs. The overarching aim of a smart city is to enhance the quality of life for its citizens through smart technology.

Social networking refers to networks or social relations among people who share similar interests, activities, backgrounds, or real-life connections. Social-networking sites allow users to share ideas, pictures, posts, activities, events, and interests with people in their network.

Examples of social networks include Facebook, Google+, LinkedIn, Instagram, Pinterest, Vine, Tumblr, and Twitter.

Valley of Death is a common term in the start-up world, referring to the difficulty of covering the negative cash flow in the early stages of a start-up before its new product or service is bringing in revenue from real customers. According to a Gompers and Lerner study, the challenge is very real, with up to 90 percent of new ventures failing within the first three years.[77]

Virtual reality (VR) describes a computer-generated 3-D environment that surrounds a user and responds to that individual's actions in a natural way, usually through immersive head-mounted displays and head tracking. Virtual reality is often confused with augmented reality, which is the real-time use of information in the form of text, graphics, audio, and other virtual enhancements integrated with real-world objects.

Wall of resistance is a new term that describes the challenges that companies and communities face from existing players within an industry or community to changes that disrupt incumbents within an industry and the status quo.

Wi-Fi is a technology that allows electronic devices to connect to a wireless local area network that exists in a contained area, like a home, business, or retail location.

Appendix II

NOTES

Leader to Leader

1. Patricia Buckley, Peter Viechnicki, and Akrur Barua, "A New Understanding of Millennials: Generational Differences Reexamined," Deloitte University Press, October 16, 2015, http://dupress.com/articles/understanding-millennials-generational-differences/.

2. "The 2016 Deloitte Millennial Survey: Winning Over the Next Generation of Leaders," https://www2.deloitte.com/content/dam/Deloitte/global/Documents/About-Deloitte/gx-millenial-survey-2016-exec-summary.pdf.

3. "The Values Revolution," Global Tolerance, 2015, http://www.globaltolerance.com/wp-content/uploads/2015/01/GT-Values-Revolution-Report.pdf.

4. DCR, "Baby Boomer Brain Drain," *DCR Trendline,* July 1, 2015, http://trendline.dcrworkforce.com/baby-boomer-brain-drain.html.

5. DCR, "Baby Boomer Brain Drain," *DCR Trendline,* July 1, 2015, http://trendline.dcrworkforce.com/baby-boomer-brain-drain.html.

The Innovation Journey

6. "Startup Business Failure Rate by Industry," *Statistic Brain,* January 24, 2016, http://www.statisticbrain.com/startup-failure-by-industry/.

7. "Survival Rates and Firm Age," SBA Office of Advocacy, 2014, https://www.sba.gov/sites/default/files/SurvivalRatesAndFirmAge_ADA_0_0.pdf.

8. "Increasing Churn Rate in the S&P 500: What's the Lifespan of Your Stock?" Seeking Alpha, November 6, 2014, http://seekingalpha.com/article/2651195-increasing-churn-rate-in-the-s-and-p-500-whats-the-lifespan-of-your-stock.

9. David Erickson, "Did You Know? Shift Happens. We Live in Exponential Times," YouTube video, 1:09, posted by *The Public Review*, December 1, 2011, https://www.youtube.com/watch?v=pRVVZlGb7oc.

10. David Erickson, "Did You Know? Shift Happens. We live in Exponential Times," YouTube video, 1:09, posted by *The Public Review*, December 1, 2011, https://www.youtube.com/watch?v=pRVVZlGb7oc.

11. Gerald C. Kane, Doug Palmer, Anh Nguyen Phillips, and David Kiron, "Is Your Business Ready for a Digital Future?" *MIT Sloan Management Review*, Summer 2015, http://sloanreview.mit.edu/article/is-your-business-ready-for-a-digital-future/.

Sparking the Innovation Engine

12. John Zarocostas, "US Again Leads in Patent Applications; University of California Is First Among Schools," March 20, 2015, http://www.mcclatchydc.com/news/nation-world/world/article24782077.html.

13. "US Extends Lead in International Patent and Trademark Filings," World Intellectual Property Organization, March 16, 2016, http://www.wipo.int/pressroom/en/articles/2016/article_0002.html.

14. "US Extends Lead in International Patent and Trademark Filings," World Intellectual Property Organization, March 16, 2016, http://www.wipo.int/pressroom/en/articles/2016/article_0002.html.

15. Martin Bailey, Jonathan Haskel, Eric Hazan, Nathan Marston, and Tamara Rajah, "McKinsey Matters, Reviving the Growth Engine," 2013, http://www.mckinsey.com/~/media/mckinsey%20offices/france/pdfs/innovation%20matters_mckinsey.ashx

16. Martin Bailey, Jonathan Haskel, Eric Hazan, Nathan Marston, and Tamara Rajah, "McKinsey Matters, Reviving the Growth Engine," 2013, http://www.mckinsey.com/~/media/mckinsey%20offices/france/pdfs/innovation%20matters_mckinsey.ashx

17. "2016 Global R&D Funding Forecast," *R&D Magazine,* Winter 2016, https://www.iriweb.org/sites/default/files/2016GlobalR%26DFundingForecast_2.pdf.

18. Matt Hourihan and David Parkes, "Federal R&D in the FY 2016 Budget: An Overview", *American Association for the Advancement of Science,* http://www.aaas.org/fy16budget/federal-rd-fy-2016-budget-overview

19. Barry Jaruzelski, Kevin Schwartz, and Volker Staack, "Innovation's New World Order," *Strategy+Business,* October 27, 2015, http://www.strategy-business.com/feature/00370?gko=e606a.

20. John Zarocostas, "US Again Leads in Patent Applications; University of California Most Among Schools," March 20, 2015, http://www.mcclatchydc.com/news/nation-world/world/article24782077.html.

Guiding Entrepreneurs through the Valley of Death

21. Zac Johnson, "Growth Stats That Contribute to Startup Success [Infographic]," *Business 2 Community,* October 10, 2015, http://www.business2community.com/infographics/growth-stats-contribute-startup-success-infographic-01349573#8RTfjWSeVI RlDcdY.97.

22. Kim Lachance Shandrow, "Where Famous Tech Founders Went to College [Infographic]," *Entrepreneur,* January 15, 2015, http://www.entrepreneur.com/article/241844.

23. "21 Facts and Statistics from 2015 Research Reports," Entrepreneurs' Organization, December 21, 2015, http://blog.eonetwork.org/2015/12/21-facts-and-statistics-from-2015-research-reports/.

24. "21 Facts and Statistics from 2015 Research Reports," Entrepreneurs' Organization, December 21, 2015, http://blog.eonetwork.org/2015/12/21-facts-and-statistics-from-2015-research-reports/.

25. "The 5 Levels of Entrepreneurship (Leveling p as an Entrepreneur)," StartupBros.com, 2013, http://startupbros.com/infographic-successful-entrepreneur-facts-stats/; EY, "Entrepreneurship Rising: Statistics from around the World," *Exceptional,* July–December 2015, http://www.ey.com/US/en/Services/Strategic-Growth-Markets/ey-exceptional-americas-july-december-2015-13-entrepreneurship-rising.

26. "Startup Companies Valued at One Billion US Dollars or More by Venture-Capital Firms Worldwide, as of June 2016, by Valuation (in Billion US Dollars)," Statista, June 2016, http://www.statista.com/statistics/407888/ranking-of-highest-valued-startup-companies-worldwide/.

27. Ian Hathaway, "Accelerating Growth: Startup Accelerator Programs in the United States," Brookings.edu, February 17, 2016, http://www.brookings.edu/research/papers/2016/02/17-startup-accelerator-programs-hathaway; Zac Johnson, "Growth Stats That Contribute to Startup Success [Infographic]," Business 2 Community, October 10, 2015, http://www.business2community.com/infographics/growth-stats-contribute-startup-success-infographic-01349573#8 RTfjWSeVIRlDcdY.97.

28. Brian Solomon, "The Best Startup Accelerators of 2016," *Forbes,* March 11, 2016, http://www.forbes.com/sites/briansolomon/2016/03/11/the-best-startup-accelerators-of-2016/#6fcddf4324f2

Navigating through Growth and Constant Change

29. David Erickson, "Did You Know? Shift Happens. We Live in Exponential Times," YouTube video, 1:09, posted by *The Public View,* December 1, 2011, https://www.youtube.com/watch?v=pRVVZlGb7oc.

30. Jake Richardson, "About $350 Billion a Year Lost Due to Unhappy Workers," Delivering Happiness.com, October 22, 2012, http://deliveringhappiness.com/350-billion-a-year-lost-due-to-unhappy-workers/.

31. Eric Kutcher, Olivia Nottebohm, and Kara Sprague, "Grow Fast or Die Slow," McKinsey & Company, April 2014, http://www.mckinsey.com/industries/high-tech/our-insights/grow-fast-or-die-slow.

32. "Today's Unicorns," Tech Crunch, June 8, 2016, http://techcrunch.com/unicorn-leaderboard/

33. Alexander Roos and Kees Cools, "The Role of Alliances in Corporate Strategy," bcg.perspectives, November 18, 2005, https://www.bcgperspectives.com/content/articles/alliance_joint_ventures_corporate_strategy_portfolio_management_the_role_of_alliances_in_corporate_strategy/.

34. "Joint Ventures and Strategic Alliances, Examining the keys to success" Pricewaterhouse Coopers, 2016, http://www.pwc.com/us/en/deals/publications/assets/pwc-deals-joint-ventures-strategic-alliances.pdf

35. "Venture Investment," National Venture Capital Association, http://nvca.org/research/venture-investment/; http://nvca.org/pressreleases/58-8-billion-in-venture-capital-invested-across-u-s-in-2015-according-to-the-moneytree-report-2/; "Stats & Studies," National Venture Capital Association, http://nvca.org/research/stats-studies/.

36. Louis Emmerson, "Crowdfunding Industry Overtakes Venture Capital and Angel Investing," Symbid.com, July 8, 2015, http://blog.symbid.com/2015/trends/crowdfunding-industry-overtakes-venture-capital-and-angel-investing/.

Evolving Despite a Wall of Resistance

37. Michelle Jamrisko, "Surge in R&D Spending Burnishes US Image as Innovation Nation," Bloomberg.com, March 26, 2015, http://www.bloomberg.com/news/articles/2015-03-26/surge-in-r-d-spending-burnishes-u-s-image-as-innovation-nation.

38. Michael Ringel, Andrew Taylor, and Hadi Zablit, "Most Innovative Companies 2015," BCG Perspectives, December 2, 2015,

https://www.bcgperspectives.com/content/articles/growth-lean-manufacturing-innovation-in-2015/.

39. "Innovation a Top Priority for Business," pwc.com, July 2, 2013, http://press.pwc.com/News-releases/innovation-a-top-priority-for-business/s/918ccaab-2d82-4889-bc41-9905b3a4b9ec.

40. Richard Florida, "The World's Leading Startup Cities," The Atlantic City Lab, July 27, 2015, http://www.citylab.com/tech/2015/07/the-worlds-leading-startup-cities/399623/.

41. "Preparing Local Economies for the Future," *Harvard Business Review,* January 12, 2016, https://hbr.org/sponsored/2016/01/preparing-local-economies-for-the-future.

Transforming Lives in the Innovation Economy

42. James Manyika, Michael Chui, Jacques Bughin, Richard Dobbs, Peter Bisson, and Alex Marrs, "Disruptive Technologies: Advances That Will Transform Life, Business, and the Global Economy," McKinsey & Company, May 2013, http://www.mckinsey.com/business-functions/business-technology/our-insights/disruptive-technologies.

43. "A Strategy for American Innovation," Whitehouse.gov, October 2015, https://www.whitehouse.gov/sites/default/files/strategy_for_american_innovation_october_2015.pdf.

44. "New Report Calculates the Size of the Internet Economy," Internet Association, December 10, 2015, https://internetassociation.org/121015econreport/.

45. "Change the World," *Fortune,* 2015, http://fortune.com/change-the-world/.

46. "USPTO Report Shows Intellectual Property-Intensive Industries Contribute $5 Trillion, 40 Million Jobs to US Economy," United States Patent and Trademark Office, January 8, 2015, http://www.uspto.gov/about-us/organizational-offices/office-policy-and-international-affairs/office-chief-economist/uspto.

47. Community Attributes Inc., "Information & Communication Technology Economic and Fiscal Impact Study," Washington Technology Industry Association, February, 2015, htp://washingtontechnology.org/wp-content/uploads/2015/04/ICT-Economic-Report.pdf?submissionGuid=46b67268-6b7a-4cf4-9e5b-bba9bd8e3614.

48. Darrell M. West, "Technology and the Innovation Economy," Brookings, October 19, 2011, http://www.brookings.edu/research/papers/2011/10/19-technology-innovation-west.

49. Power of Purpose-Driven…Business, Leadership, Management: Focus on-Reason to Exist, Vision, Mission-It Really Matters," BizShifts-Trends, February 3, 2014, http://bizshifts-trends.com/2014/02/03/power-purpose-driven-business-leadership-management-focus-mission-vision-reason-exist-really-matters/.

50. P. Kotter, "Corporate Culture and Performance," Free Press, May 16, 2011, http://www.amazon.com/Corporate-Culture-Performance-John-Kotter/dp/1451655320.

Engaging in the Innovation Economy—Are You Ready?

51. "2015–2016 Dice Salary Survey," Dice, January 26, 2016, http://media.dice.com/report/2015-2016-dice-salary-survey/.

52. Stacy Rapacon, "The 10 Hottest Careers for the Next 10 Years," Kiplinger, Spring 2016, http://www.kiplinger.com/slideshow/business/T012-S001-best-jobs-for-the-future-2016/index.html.

53. James Manyika, Sree Ramaswamy, Somesh Khanna, Hugo Sarrazin, Gary Pinkus, Guru Sethupathy, and Andrew Yaffe, "Digital America: A Tale of the Haves and Have-Mores," McKinsey Global Institute, December 2015, http://www.mckinsey.com/industries/high-tech/our-insights/digital-america-a-tale-of-the-haves-and-have-mores.

54. C. Kane, Doug Palmer, Anh Nguyen Phillips, and David Kiron, "Is Your Business Ready for a Digital Future?" MIT Sloan Management Review, Summer 2015, http://sloanreview.mit.edu/article/is-your-business-ready-for-a-digital-future/.

55. Swabey, "Business Leaders Optimistic about the Fourth Industrial Revolution's Impact on Jobs," The Economist, January 21, 2016, http://www.eiuperspectives.economist.com/technology-innovation/business-leaders-optimistic-about-fourth-industrial-revolution%E2%80%99s-impact-jobs.

56. Vincent, "Innovation and the Impact on Future Jobs," LinkedIn, September 3, 2015, https://www.linkedin.com/pulse/innovation-impact-future-jobs-john-vincent.

57. "A Marketplace without Boundaries? Responding to Disruption," pwc.com, January 2015, http://www.pwc.com/gx/en/ceo-survey/2015/assets/pwc-18th-annual-global-ceo-survey-jan-2015.pdf.

58. SHRM Foundation, "The Cratering of the Middle Class[Infographic]," The Economist, http://futurehrtrends.eiu.com/infographics/the-cratering-of-the-middle-class/.

59. Mary Meeker, "Internet Trends 2016—Code Conference," KPCB.com, June 1, 2016, http://www.kpcb.com/internet-trends.

60. Mary Meeker, "Internet Trends 2016—Code Conference," KPCB.com, June 1, 2016, http://www.kpcb.com/internet-trends.

61. James Manyika, Michael Chui, Jacques Bughin, Richard Dobbs, Peter Bisson, and Alex Marrs, "Disruptive Technologies: Advances That Will Transform Life, Business, and the Global Economy," May 2013, http://www.mckinsey.com/business-functions/business-technology/our-insights/disruptive-technologies.

Post Script

62. Jim Clifton, "American Entrepreneurship: Dead or Alive?" Gallup, January 13, 2015, http://www.gallup.com/business-journal/180431/american-entrepreneurship-dead-alive.aspx.

Appendix I: Glossary of Frequently Used Innovation Terms

63. IT Glossary, Gartner.com, 2016, http://www.gartner.com/it-glossary/b.

64. Encyclopedia, PCMag Digital Group, 2016, http://www.pcmag.com/encyclopedia/index/a.

65. Dictionary, Techopedia, 2016, https://www.techopedia.com/.

66. *Wikipedia,* 2016, https://en.wikipedia.org/wiki/Main_Page.

67. "Definition of Pivot," *Financial Times,* http://lexicon.ft.com/Term?term=pivot.

68. Reference Dictionary, 2016, http://www.investopedia.com/dictionary/.

69. Paul Zwillenberg, Dominic Field, and David Dean, "The Connected World: Greasing the Wheels of the Internet Economy," The Boston Consulting Group, January 2014, https://www.icann.org/en/system/files/files/bcg-internet-economy-27jan14-en.pdf.

70. Wenstrup, Joel Janda, and Shawn Collins, "Perspectives on Seattle as a Globally Competitive Region," The Boston Consulting Group, August 2014, https://www.bcg.com/documents/file166072.pdf.

71. "Innovation District," *Wikipedia,* https://en.wikipedia.org/wiki/Innovation_district.

72. Bruce Katz and Julie Wagner, "The Rise of Innovation Districts: A New Geography of Innovation in America," Brookings, 2014, http://www.brookings.edu/about/programs/metro/innovation-districts.

73. Tuukka Toivonen and Nicolas Friederici, "Time to Define What a 'Hub' Really Is," *Stanford Social Innovation Review,* April 7, 2015, http://ssir.org/articles/entry/time_to_define_what_a_hub_really_is.

74. "Definition of Pivot," *Financial Times,* http://lexicon.ft.com/Term?term=pivot.

75. "Building the Digital Platform: Insights from the 2016 Gartner CIO Agenda Report," Gartner, 2016, https://www.gartner.com/imagesrv/cio/pdf/cio_agenda_insights_2016.pdf.

76. "Platform Economy: Technology-Driven Business Model Innovation from the Outside In," Accenture, 2016, https://www.

accenture.com/t20160125T111719__w__/us-en/_acnmedia/
Accenture/Omobono/TechnologyVision/pdf/Platform-
Economy-Technology-Vision-2016.pdf#zoom=50.

77. Martin Zwilling, "10 Ways for Startups to Survive the Valley of
Death," *Forbes,* February 18, 2013, http://www.forbes.com/sites/
martinzwilling/2013/02/18/10-ways-for-startups-to-survive-
the-valley-of-death/#29a7f4ed5e40

Author Biography

Randy Ottinger is a technology entrepreneur, author, and thought leader in the areas of business leadership and innovation. He has worked for top technology companies including IBM and McCaw Cellular, as well as venture-backed technology companies. In addition, Ottinger cofounded Kotter International with Harvard Business School professor, John Kotter, a management consulting firm specializing in leadership, innovation, and organizational change. His latest venture is the iInnovate Leadership Network, a peer-to-peer CEO network for innovators and entrepreneurs.

Ottinger is the author of *Beyond Success: Building a Personal, Financial, and Philanthropic Legacy.* His blog posts and articles have appeared in *Forbes, Chief Executive Magazine,* and the *Financial Times,* among other top media. In addition, with the support of the University of Washington, he has published studies that deepen our understanding of business innovation networks and community ecosystems.

Ottinger is passionate about improving lives through innovation and entrepreneurship. He has a BA from Cornell University and an MBA from Harvard's Graduate School of Business. He is happily married with three grown children, and lives in Seattle.